MANAGING HUMAN RESOURCES IN CALL CENTRES

NICK GARRETT, TERRY JACQUES AND BERNARD WYNNE

First published in 2002 by
Spiro Press
17–19 Rochester Row
London
SW1P 1LA
Telephone: +44 (0)870 400 1000

© N. Garrett, T. Jacques and B. Wynne, 2002

ISBN 1 904298 52 4

Reprinted October 2002
Ref 6037.JC.10.2002

British Library Cataloguing-in-Publication Data.
A catalogue record for this book is available from the British Library.

Spiro Press USA
3 Front Street, Suite 331
PO Box 338
Rollinsford NH 03869
USA

Printed in Great Britain by: Biddles, UK
Cover design by: REAL451

MANAGING HUMAN RESOURCES
IN CALL CENTRES

SPIRO BUSINESS GUIDES
HUMAN RESOURCES AND TRAINING

Spiro Business Guides are designed to provide managers with practical, down-to-earth information, and they are written by leading authors in their respective fields. If you would like to receive a full listing of current and forthcoming titles, please visit www.spiropress.com or email spiropress@capita-ld.co.uk or call us on +44 (0)870 400 1000.

New authors: we are always pleased to receive ideas for new titles; if you would like to write a Spiro Business Guide, please contact Dr Glyn Jones at spiropress@capita-ld.co.uk or call direct on +44 (0)1865 884447.

Bulk orders: some organisations buy a number of copies of our books. If you are interested in doing this, we would be pleased to discuss a discount. Please contact the Customer Centre on +44 (0)870 400 1000 or email spiropress@capita-ld.co.uk.

Contents

Introduction

It seems that every time you telephone any organisation large or small, your call is likely to be routed through a call centre. Ten, perhaps even five years ago, the number of call centres in the UK were few and far between. They now proliferate. Everyone wants one, everyone runs one, yet real experience of establishing and managing a call centre is understandably limited. There is only a limited pool of managers with experience of establishing and managing call centres which organisations can dip into.

Much recent publicity about call centres has suggested that they are sweatshops established in areas of high unemployment, that they employ people with low skills, offer little in the way of training or advancement for employees and suffer from a high employee turnover. Organisations, however, continue to invest considerable sums in establishing call centres and there is little doubt that call centres are here to stay. The number is increasing daily, resulting in an increased demand for managers and others associated with call centres to become aware of and develop the special skills required in managing them.

Call centres, by definition, are people-intensive operations and it is becoming increasingly clear that how agents are managed on a daily basis greatly influences the effectiveness of the operation.

Drawing on experience of working in a number of call centres in the UK and on published research and experience in North America, this practical book will help those tasked with managing the human resource in call centres review some of the important issues they need to address.

About the authors

Nick Garrett has spent his career in financial services where his time has been divided between the design and delivery of management training programmes and the provision of in-house human resources consultancy.

He is a regular speaker at conferences and seminars, and a contributor to books and articles on topics including performance management within call centres and effective remuneration strategies for sales people. He is co-author with Bernard Wynne of a management report *Training and the Bottom Line.*

Terry Jacques, following early experience in engineering and retail management, has spent over 25 years specialising in HR and training within the financial services industry. His experience ranges from the provision of 'front-line' HR services to senior management and a position as group training and development manager at a time of unprecedented change in the industry.

He was involved in the setting up of a call centre in the 'early days', preparing the organisation for the transition from mutual to PLC status and its successful reaccredidation for Investors in People. He recently completed a strategic review of call centre training for a UK bank. He is a business partner and training consultant with IMB Training Services who specialise in communication, customer service, sales training and management development particularly for the call centre industry.

Bernard Wynne is principal of Bernard Wynne Associates, an independent consultancy. He has worked as a consultant since 1988 and is employed widely in the areas of HR, management development and performance management across all business sectors. He has considerable experience of working with managers worldwide in the development of personal skills.

He writes extensively on HR and management development topics and has contributed to chapters in *The Handbook of Training and Development* and *The Handbook of Management Development.* He has written Management Briefings published by Financial Times on *Performance Appraisal* and with David Stringer *A Competency Based Approach to Training and Development.*

The authors can be contacted at:

IMB Training Services

4 Hillcrest Road

Orpington

Kent

BR6 9AW

Tel/fax: 01689 836431

Mobile: 07979 950284

Email: terryjacques1@aol.com

CHAPTER 1

What do you expect from your call centre?

Why are call centres so popular?

Increasing numbers of organisations are implementing and expanding call centres as part of a strategy to improve their customer service, as well as increase potential productivity. The number of call centres in the UK has grown beyond expectation in recent years, together with the number of people employed in what has become the fastest growing industry. It is estimated that more than 2% of the UK workforce are now involved in call centres. Over £1.8 billion was spent on call centre computer equipment in 1999 – up from £300 million in 1994.

So what exactly do we mean when we use the term Call Centre? It is often loosely used to describe a variety of telephone operations but particularly a group of employees (generally referred to as agents, a title we use throughout this book) whose primary role is answering and/or making telephone calls. Call centres ultimately consist of two components: electronic equipment (a computer screen and integrated headset) and people. The former must empower the latter to act in the company's best interests.

Call centres vary greatly in terms of size, from a handful of people to thousands based at a single or multi-site operation. The technology and telephony available makes it possible for customers to be seamlessly transferred from one centre to another, possibly hundreds of miles away, as the situation requires.

As the popularity of call centres in the UK has increased so too have the comments about the general level of service they provide to customers and the conditions and pressures some staff work under. The quality and speed with which calls are handled are important measures of how an organisation performs from the caller's point of view. Callers who are kept waiting may hang up and take their business elsewhere. Lost calls mean lost business and, in many instances, customers lost forever. Without an effective call centre, an organisation may not even be aware of the scale of the potential business loss.

Old industries – new ways of doing business

There has been a growing acceptance in Britain of the telephone as a form of communication. We are finally catching up with America, Canada, Hong Kong, Japan and Australia where it has been a dominant communications medium for quite some time. Technology aside, the potential benefits to companies and customers are so great today that most businesses are expected to have some form of telephony-based customer service. Businesses can increase professionalism and maximise productivity by simply improving access at the front end.

Organisations and industries where the use of call centres have become most widespread are those where the focus is on customer service and a high volume of dispersed customer contact, such as:

- banking and finance;

- insurance;

- airlines;

- telecommunications;

- travel services;

- road services;

- emergency services;

- mail order companies;

- sharedealing;

- public utilities.

However, this is only a random selection as the list is growing all the time. Even the Inland Revenue in a recent advertisement for a Director of Call Centres said that they were adopting a radical new approach to customer service. They were introducing call centres, seating up to 500 people each, which should become the first port of call for customers on all tax-related issues.

Why organisations choose call centres

There are many reasons for such companies to utilise a call centre:

- Call centres can deliver improved customer service by increasing access for customers and allowing for more rapid completion of enquires and transactions.

- Call centres can provide access to services for customers at a time to suit them and their twenty-first century lifestyle. Customers of insurance companies, banks, travel agents and mail order companies are increasingly seeking advice without obligation and demand the opportunity to make a quick call and a spontaneous decision to purchase on the phone.

- Call centres can facilitate the rationalisation of operations through the removal of significant volumes of customer enquiries and the re-engineering of transactions. Call centres can be located anywhere and the concentration of customer enquiries in a single, or small, number of centres enables economies of scale in staffing and related costs.

- Call centres can reorganise transactions by redirecting telephone traffic and enabling the remaining branches to specialise in providing specific services or sales for walk-in customers.

Major cost savings

However, perhaps the greatest impetus driving the growth of call centres has been the significant cost saving they can deliver.

- Studies into the relative cost of face-to-face operations and call centre operations have shown that a call centre can deliver substantial benefits in relation to the cost. Customer contact through the use of the telephone has the potential to significantly lower operational costs compared to over-the-counter/face-to-face services. Telephone costs are less than the provision of counter services where there is a large volume of customer contact with consistent and predictable responses to issues not requiring face-to-face contact. Call centres are increasingly used to complement existing distribution channels and give the customer choice, particularly in the industries referred to above.

- There is also a noticeable shift as call centres move from being cost centres to profit centres. What started, for many call centres, as just the provision of 'help desk' style information now sees the service moving rapidly to the provision of a wide variety of inbound and outbound sales and marketing activity. Call centres enable many organisations to undertake a much more proactive approach to product distribution and the meeting of customer needs.

- Dealing directly with customers can cut out the middleman, which in turn reduces costs and improves efficiency. Enquiries can be answered immediately, complaints dealt with instantly and delivery turned around in less than 24 hours.

- Agents who have access to a vast bank of customer information, instantly available at the touch of a button, can use this information to introduce new and additional products and services to customers.

Many organisations that have ventured down the call centre route were undoubtedly influenced by the success of Direct Line, who by tapping into the potential of telephony-based sales and marketing transformed the world of home and motor insurance. They are living proof that the simplest ideas really can be the best.

Although there are substantial benefits to be gained from the establishment of call centres, as previously described, they require a significant investment in terms of technology, people and time. While it must be for each individual organisation to undertake its own cost-benefit analysis to establish a sound economic and business case before making a decision to establish a call centre, it can be said that many organisations have achieved significant cost savings as a result of moving part of their operation to a call centre.

Challenges and opportunities in managing a call centre

Views vary on whether or not the management issues in call centres are different from those in other work environments. Due to the highly technical and monitored nature of most call centres a unique set of stresses affect the people who work in them. What is beyond doubt is that such unique conditions have to be taken into account by call centre managers and supervisors. Particular factors

concerning motivation and morale in call centres will be discussed later.

What is universally agreed is that people are the essential ingredient that drives the success or otherwise of call centres. An organisation may have the best possible environment and state-of-the-art technology but if it does not get the people management issues right then it will never release the full potential of the people who are the key to the success of any call centre operation.

Call centre managers and supervisors/team leaders need to be carefully recruited and selected against clearly defined criteria. The most successful agent does not always make the best supervisor – no surprise there! But the knowledge, skills, attitude and behaviour of supervisors in call centres drives the performance of the agents. Performance management will be discussed in more detail later but the ability of the supervisor to monitor and observe calls, with or without call-recording facilities, and to assess the agents' performance, give feedback and coach are all critical factors. To do this on a regular basis, perhaps as a targeted percentage of their time, is a major challenge for managers to enforce, as there always seems to be other things to do! Getting this right is a key element in running a really successful call centre.

Using call-recording facilities

Where call-recording facilities exist they are not always used to good effect. Although they provide protection in the event of a complaint and prove that certain legal/security requirements were dealt with, the potential benefits from call monitoring, coaching and performance improvement are often wasted. For a supervisor to listen to recorded calls and then give feedback to the agent can be time consuming, but it is time well spent. Alternatively there are a number of companies who take a random sample of recorded calls per agent per month and outsource the analysis. In this way the outsource company provides reports on each call, analysed against predetermined criteria. Consistency then applies across all teams and the supervisor can then coach their agents through each call analysed, building skills and working towards performance improvement.

Supervisors and agents need to understand very clearly their respective roles and responsibilities and what the major priorities are for them, their boss and the call centre. Communication of the targets and performance of the centre – and more importantly the vision management has for the call centre – can be a major challenge. Get it right and it turns into another opportunity! Getting it wrong, however, can mean failing to capitalise on the benefit that the people can bring to the operation. The environment can be so fast moving and the learning curve so steep that basic communication can very often suffer. This in itself can be a major frustration for agents and may have an adverse impact on their performance.

Multi-skilling

As with supervisors, recruitment, induction and ongoing training and development for agents is critical. Multi-skilling has become the norm – it provides flexibility and helps reduce boredom for agents, thus contributing to higher morale and improved performance. Repetition of tasks can be a serious issue for agents and can affect their morale and motivation, as well as how long they remain employed. Trying to keep their work interesting, competitive and fun can be a big challenge but, as many have proved, can be achieved. This together with creating a supportive, coaching culture can help to ensure a high performing team.

Very often the contact with the call centre is the only contact the customer has with the organisation. This presents a great opportunity from which managers can learn. By listening in to calls they can get the feel for:

- what motivates the customer;

- how the agent is dealing with the customer;

- pick up valuable 'intelligence' and customer feedback.

Sadly such opportunities are often overlooked by call centre managers as they juggle with the priorities and demands of day-to-day management issues.

The accessibility of information and customer history, if the technology is in place, presents an ideal opportunity to excel in terms of customer service and, where appropriate, to cross sell and upsell other products and services. Going the extra mile in terms of customer service can make a major difference to the ongoing relationship with the customer.

What goes wrong?

As has been stated before call centres have not always enjoyed the best of press. Research by the Henley Centre Consultancy claims that 'one in ten calls leave customers feeling irritated, anxious or furious'.

Major irritants for customers include:

- limited and restricted hours of business;

- impersonal service from apparently disinterested agents;

- trying to deal with an endless maze of automatic responses, except the one they want;

- automatic response systems, which are not user-friendly;

- the failure to obtain satisfactory answers to their questions;

- queuing without being told how long they will have to wait;

- the sheer irritation of not being able to speak to another human being.

From an employee viewpoint issues that cause irritation include:

- chronic shortages of staff;

- low levels of employee retention;

- low pay;

- uncomfortable, inadequate working conditions;

- pressurised working conditions.

The image created by views and opinions such as those above expressed by customers and employees is one that call centre managers need to be acutely aware of and work hard to overcome.

Quality and quantity

Perhaps the biggest challenge of all for call centre managers is balancing the sometimes conflicting issues of quantity and quality. In many call centre environments call times are targeted and closely monitored and it becomes ingrained as part of the culture. This can frequently work against achieving customer service excellence if the agent is trying to keep the call as short as possible, with one eye on the number of calls in the queue. The opportunity to delight the customer is frequently lost in a culture where reactivity takes precedence over proactivity.

Avoiding the pitfalls and overcoming the difficulties

One of the most effective ways of avoiding the pitfalls is to learn from others and the mistakes they have made. Very often a call centre operation is being set up within one part of an organisation, which may already have a call centre elsewhere within the business. Networking and internally benchmarking with the key players in the parts of the business that already has some call centre experience to find out what went well and not so well can provide real benefit and avoid much frustration. It is important for managers to avoid having to reinvent the wheel. Many people issues will be the same or similar, particularly issues of recruitment, training, performance management, standards and competencies.

The pace of change within the industry is accelerating all the time so networking outside of the organisation, as well as inside, will pay dividends. Keep up to date via call centre magazines and journals and the Internet, and by attending appropriate workshops and seminars.

Another way that organisations can avoid pitfalls and overcome difficulties is to participate in benchmarking projects in order to see how their organisation compares against the industry as a whole.

Benchmarking is rapidly becoming one of the most significant business tools for performance improvement, through setting standards for systems and operational procedures which improve efficiency and customer service.

In the call centre industry, benchmarking represents an opportunity to see how an organisation matches others on a series of key performance indicators. It allows comparisons of individual performance against best practice. A benchmarking exercise can identify strengths and weaknesses, as well as offer a learning experience to develop and monitor progress over time.

Benchmarking projects concentrate on a small number of generic measures common across industries and call centre functions. Categories where benchmarking can help include:

* resource management:

    – overflow load;

    – agent efficiency;

    – occupancy rate;

- personnel management:
  - mix of agents;
  - agent turnover;
  - early leaver rate;
  - absenteeism;
  - bonus schemes;
  - training;
  - reporting ratio;
- operational performance:
  - average speed of call answer;
  - threshold service factor;
  - abandoned call rate;
  - abandoned call time;
  - percentage of calls engaged;
- telecommunication costs:
  - inbound calls;
  - outbound calls.

Once data has been collected work needs to be done to identify best practice and a report prepared.

Establishing the vision and values

For effective call centre operation it is essential to have a clear strategy in place with specific objectives that are realistic in terms of achievement and timescales. The associated vision and values should be clear and understood by all from top to bottom. Not knowing where the call centre is going and how it is going to get there can be the source of frustration and demotivation for supervisors and agents alike.

As with any venture or development the degree of success can only be measured if the starting point is known. The call centre operation must be measurable and evaluated in order for implementation to be a success. The actual measures and expectations of what constitutes success will differ from one organisation to another, therefore the long-term goals designed to measure success need to be in place and well communicated at the start.

One specific pitfall for call centre managers is not managing the organisation's expectations against resource availability, which in turn can put customer service levels at risk. There are many horror stories around call traffic far exceeding resourcing, particularly with start up operations.

With share dealing services, for example, the volume of calls is driven by interest rates and market factors when time is of the essence for customers. In some instances it has been necessary to produce newsletters for customers to explain the situation and what is being done to speed up the service in the future. Clearly where call traffic can be volatile contingency arrangements need to be made so that additional resources can be 'turned on' when the need arises.

Management information overload

Another common pitfall is management information overload. The system can be so sophisticated and produce so much information that can be 'sliced and diced' in a range of different ways. The focus should be on reports that provide information that help to improve business and agent performance, not information for information's sake. If this is to be achieved managers need to stand back and think about what information is available. Out of what is available they need to identify the specific information that will enable them to manage the business more effectively and discard information that only contributes to effectiveness in a peripheral way. Our experience suggests that placing a focus on information that can make a difference to customer service and business improvement, rather than falling into the trap of gathering too much information is likely to be more effective.

Achieving this is not easy and requires management discipline and the development of a clearly defined reporting infrastructure, which adds value to the business rather than putting pressure on supervisors to master the stunning array of customer management tools which are available.

The people factor

Given that 70% of the annual cost of running a call centre are employee costs, it is critical that managers and supervisors ensure that the operation gets maximum value from this investment. Many call centres suffer from above average levels of staff turnover. For many the average length of service is only 31 months and the average age of employees is 28, therefore every effort must be made to utilise the people resource as effectively as possible. This is discussed in more detail later in this book, but of now it is important to stress that robust systems for recruitment, training, development and performance management are all essential ingredients together with an ongoing management and employee development programme.

Many call centres require agents to use prepared scripts in their interactions with callers. If this is the case it is paramount that agents and supervisors ensure that any scripting requirements for legal and security reasons are complied with. While agents should be trained to deliver most scripting or screen prompts in their own words and personality, however, they should not deviate from any mandatory or regulatory requirements.

While call centres have the capacity to streamline operations and provide efficiencies, they also have the potential to place a drain on the organisation if not effectively and comprehensively planned, implemented and managed. Furthermore, experience has shown that it can be a long and costly process to fix and recover from mistakes. If for this and no other reason it is essential to make sure that careful planning and a cost-benefit analysis precedes the implementation of any call centre.

Establishing key priorities, goals and values and linking them to the vision for business success

Initially it is safe to assume that some if not all key priorities and goals for the call centre will have been predetermined. They will form part of the overall strategic plan for the business and especially the part of the business to be covered by the operation of the call centre.

The key measures are likely to take the form of hard measures based around the performance of the call centre over the succeeding one, two and three years. They will include items such as business volumes, income generated, costs to run the business, profit, growth targets, employee satisfaction and, of course, customer satisfaction. Dependencies will be built in, such as links to other parts of the business for whom the call centre is providing a complementary service.

While some or all of the above goals and priorities may be a 'given' and the organisation will have expectations of the local management of the call centre, beyond that it will be for local management to determine how the objectives are to be achieved, the interim steps along the way and especially the values and vision that will underpin the operation. When establishing a call centre it can be helpful to pose and answer a number of questions:

- What is the vision for the organisation?

- How does this relate to the role of local management?

- What is the local management vision for the call centre?

- What are the real issues to be faced?

- What needs to change in order to achieve the vision?

- What values should be weaved into the call centre environment?

- What are the current strengths, weaknesses, opportunities and threats for the call centre in general and the management team in particular.

Some or all of the answers to these questions should help local management to plot a course for how they are going to achieve their objectives.

Determining the vision

Determining the vision of local management for the call centre can take considerable time and effort. It will certainly be important to consult widely with all those to be involved, in identifying cultural values.

It will be important to have a clear picture of the 'perfect day'. Once the vision has been achieved what will be happening in the call centre, what does local management expect to see, hear and feel?

Once the vision has been determined it is necessary to work out what needs to be done, by whom and by when if the call centre is to get there. Finally the vision needs to be clearly communicated to all supervisors and agents. Everyone needs to understand where the operation is going and why, the priorities, the key issues and what is expected of them. The vision, the ownership and buy-in to it will be the foundation on which everything else is built. Everyone working in the call centre, from top to bottom, should be able to articulate the vision and live the values.

As previously stated supervisors and managers will be critical to achieving the key priorities and goals, building on the strengths and overcoming the weaknesses. It will only be through them that the vision will be achieved. The attitude and behaviour of senior management will have a major impact on them, which in turn will affect their attitude and behaviour and the attitude and behaviour of their teams.

The style of management throughout the call centre will influence the culture and determine the values. If openness, honesty, mutual respect, fairness and a consultative culture are desired outcomes, then managers and supervisors must understand that and lead by example, modelling the behaviour accordingly. The focus should be on looking to catch people doing something right, giving praise and recognition, as well as sharing and celebrating success.

All employees need to have the opportunity for ongoing training and development, the chance to progress, room to grow and multi-skill, and they must be aware that all these things are possible and will be supported. Do they feel they are allowed to say what they think, that they will be listened to and action taken? A reality check from time to time by way of an employee satisfaction survey may help to benchmark the progress being made.

However successful the business, every call centre will experience employee turnover, but establishing the values described above will help to keep it below the norm.

One of the key values will surely be around customer service and the desire to be known for customer service excellence. This desire should be embedded in the culture and not just a bolt on. Everyone has to buy into it, believe it and want to deliver it day in and day out. The focus should not be on customer satisfaction measures but the provision of excellent customer service all the time. Achieve this and the figures will look after themselves. However, high targets, increasing call volumes and demanding customers will remain a constant issue and need to be carefully managed if the goals are to be achieved.

Cost control will always be an issue for call centre managers, although generally speaking call centres are low-cost providers relative to other distribution channels with the exception of the Internet. People costs represent the lion's share of most call centre operational costs and will always need to be carefully managed to avoid budget overrun.

Delivering customer satisfaction

Customers in the twenty-first century have expectations far in excess of what was experienced ever before. They are more demanding than ever, not afraid to complain and are always prepared to vote with their feet. There is plenty of competition out there ready and waiting to pick up lost customers. In ensuring customer satisfaction call centre managers should ask:

• How important is good customer service to my operation?

• How good are we at it?

• How can we improve?

• What service level agreements are in place and do we meet them?

• How do we measure customer satisfaction?

• What customer service training have the team had?

• How good are we at dealing with difficult customers and complaints?

• What are our relationships like with other parts of the business?

If the answer to one or more is 'I don't know' then read on and consider the following:

- If we don't look after our customers then somebody else will.

- It takes months to find a customer and seconds to lose one.

- On average every satisfied customer tells three others.

- On average every dissatisfied customer tells ten others.

The potential cost of lost business is phenomenal. Every business claims to place a high value on customer satisfaction. Unfortunately for many it remains a slogan or a poster on a wall and frequently fails to get translated into the delivery of excellent customer service. Achieving success requires a genuine desire from top to bottom to really delight the customer every time and make contact with the organisation a memorable experience. It is not just about achieving targeted customer satisfaction measures but making customer service excellence an ingrained part of the day-to-day activity. This needs to be clearly understood by all employees and encompassed as part of the vision.

Making service excellent

A range of things needs to be considered to ensure the delivery of excellent customer service, including:

- the quality of the agents recruited and the focus given to customer service during their training;

- the regular use of call recording and monitoring to ensure that the quality of calls remains high;

- targeted rostering to ensure availability of staff at peak times, which will probably require the use of part-time staff;

- is the technology user-friendly for agents and does it provide accurate customer information? New callers should be identified and greeted as such. Menus and choices should be regularly reviewed when customers are using touch tone phones to select options;

- queue lengths, call time lengths and quality, abandonment rates and predictions of call volumes should all appear regularly on management reports;

- after-sales/service quality, speed of administration and accuracy of paperwork sent out should all be monitored, with a diary system for follow-up calls to quality check service or to look at other customer needs, e.g. renewal dates.

Measuring customer satisfaction

Customer satisfaction can be measured in a variety of ways, including:

- a check by the agent at the end of the call to ensure that the customer received all the information they wanted;

- follow-up calls after a few days by a manager or an outsource company to evaluate customer satisfaction;

- regular customer questionnaires and surveys;

- volume of repeat business received;

- level of complaints received;

- declination rates, e.g. with add-on items such as extended warranties or protection insurance;

- volume of referral opportunities identified by service agents and whether or not the hand off was successful;

- volume of business from recommendations.

The ultimate measure of course is overall performance and the business success of the operation.

The people factor

However good the company is, however well organised and equipped the call centre might be, at the end of the day it's the agents that make the difference.

- Has the training they received been transferred to the workplace?

- Are agents skilled at establishing and maintaining rapport with the customer, asking the right questions and listening to the answers?

- Can they put themselves in the customer's shoes?

- Are agents advocates of the company's products and services? If not why not?

- Can agents deal effectively with difficult customers?

- Do agents treat customers as customers and not just another phone call, form or piece of paper?

- Do agents 'wow' the customers they are in contact with?

If the answer to all to these questions is not yes there is still some way to go in delivering complete customer satisfaction, let alone exceeding their expectations. The interaction between the agent and the customer is what really matters when it comes to customer satisfaction.

Devising, communicating and implementing a style for managing people

To a large extent the appropriate management and leadership style will have started to emerge from the issues considered in the earlier section covering priorities, goals, values and vision. Call centre work can be intensive and results driven and the management style should take this into account in creating an environment where the agents want to come to work, enjoy what they do and get satisfaction from it.

It is important for agents to be equally as bright and enthusiastic with the last customer of the shift as they were with the first. Each call presents them with a unique challenge whether it's a service call or sales call. The management and leadership style adopted by managers and supervisors will heavily influence their attitude and behaviour to customers.

If you want an open and honest environment everyone needs to be aware that this is the case. Managers and supervisors must practise what they preach – actions speak far louder than words. Happy staff usually means happy customers but there are limits to what is and isn't acceptable. Fun can be introduced into the workplace provided the process remains business like and appropriate. It can relieve the tendency towards boredom.

However, staff must understand the consequences of below par performance or unacceptable behaviour.

The organisational structure must be clear for all to see as well as the communications channels both up and down. Team performances should be reviewed daily, success celebrated and targets, if they exist, communicated. Frequency of call observations and monitoring need to be clearly understood as well as the approach to performance management. This may seem excessive control to some but is a key feature of call centres in general.

Team meetings with supervisors need to be held on a regular basis and in turn the supervisors should follow this with meetings with their own teams. First-class, open communication should be high on everyone's agenda. A detailed process for communication in a call centre is provided later in this book.

Likewise, the frequency of formal performance reviews should be known by everyone and meetings booked well in advance.

Getting results through people

Managers and supervisors should have a very clear understanding of their role and responsibilities, as well as the impact that their day-to-day attitude and behaviour can have on each other and their teams. They must know what is expected of them and that it will be measured, as well as appreciating how critical performance management is. Managing performance is an essential element to include in every manager's objectives. Targets and systems should be in place and widely communicated to ensure measurement of success.

In some call centres supervisors are expected to spend 70–80% of their time on performance management and coaching. Supervisors and agents should understand that performance management is the norm and they have nothing to fear from it and everything to gain. Quality feedback and coaching can only improve their performance of the agent – and in many cases the earning potential!

The criteria for performance management should be clearly understood with standards set around frequency of observation, observation forms, competencies, call structure, scoring, etc. Everyone should know that call length is not the only measurement but that quality is important as well! Training and development needs can be identified from call monitoring which can assist further career progression.

Most coaching will inevitably come from supervisors but it is a good idea to generate a coaching culture where everyone can take on this role. This may be difficult for some to accept, as the need for coaching can be viewed as implied criticism. However, if everyone accepts it's all right to coach and be coached then a true coaching ethos can prevail.

Hot-desking, the practice of each individual not having a set desk or particular place to sit, can significantly help with the coaching culture as agents move around and sit alongside different colleagues who will have varying strengths and development needs.

Before taking live calls agents must achieve a predetermined level of competence and be confirmed as being competent through a recognised process. If this minimal level of competence is not achieved remedial training may be necessary. This issue is discussed in more detail later in the book.

Some organisations operate a red/amber/green approach to their competencies.

- Red coloured competencies represent those competencies that are considered essential to have before agents are allowed to deal directly with customers.

- Amber coloured competencies represent competencies that can be developed in the short term.

- Green coloured competencies represent competencies that agents are expected to develop in the longer term.

A structured approach to building the skills required by agents is essential for the effective operation of a call centre. Given the relatively high employee turnover in many call centres the training and development of both existing and new employees is an ongoing requirement which, if neglected, is likely to be quickly reflected in the performance measures of the call centre.

Training and development is discussed in more detail in Chapter 4 of this book and an outline for some essential training programmes has been provided.

Whatever management style is adopted it is essential that everyone in the call centre knows where they stand and what is expected of them. The attitude and behaviour of everyone will rub off on others and it is essential for the management team to lead by example. After all, behaviour breeds behaviour!

Checklist of key actions

- The environment and technology are extremely important but it's the people who drive the quality of the transaction and the final outcome of the call.

- Management practices must take account of the unique qualities, demands and characteristics of working by telephone. Practices should include forecasting of call loads and patterns, flexible staffing to meet uneven demand, regular work observation, monitoring of staff development, quality control, strong leadership and employee participation.

- Strike a balance between the intense and results-driven nature of call centre work and a working environment where staff are happy and want to be there.

- Assess the starting point and measure the performance of agents, supervisors and the call centre overall on a regular basis.

- Get the targets and balance right between quality and quantity.

- Network within the organisation as well as externally, and consider benchmarking your call centre.

- Avoid management information overload.

- Maximise the use of call recording facilities, if available, for monitoring, coaching and training.

- Create a coaching culture.

- Develop a customer service ethos that takes account of twenty-first century customer expectations.

- Create a vision, communicate it and live it.

CHAPTER 2

Working structure, performance and rewards

Agreeing the structure and working practices

The term 'call centre' encompasses such a bewildering variety of business types, purposes and functions that it appears unlikely that any general observations concerning structure and working practices could be helpful. Given, however, that the media are all too ready to present them as 'modern-day sweat shops' getting the structure and working practices correct are vital ingredients in ensuring that a call centre is capable of running efficiently and effectively. It is worth exploring what has led to the appearance of the commonly used expression 'sweat shop', and why the call centre environment is perceived to be somehow different from the norm.

In the study of articles critical of call centres will be found references to:

- poor rates of pay;

- unpleasant or cramped working conditions;

- inadequate investment in training;

- aggressive management practices.

All of these are issues that could potentially be raised in relation to any organisation or working environment. The reasons for the 'bad press' associated with call centres do not lie here. There are, however, two further themes that emerge which are of greater significance. These are:

- the repetitive nature of the work;

- the pressure of a closely targeted environment.

This is not to suggest that all call centres share these problems, as clearly this would be too great a generalisation. What can be stated, however, is that many call centres are based upon the twin objectives of improving customer service while at the same time reducing costs. These can be difficult goals to reconcile.

The structure of a call centre, and the methods of working taking place within it, will be influenced by a number of factors including:

- *Purpose.* This relates to the complexity and variety of the work taking place, including such issues as whether the operation can be perceived as a cost centre or profit centre.

- *Origination.* The circumstances that led to the creation of a call centre can have a huge influence on its structure and working practices. A number of options are possible:

New location New staff	New location Existing staff
Existing location New staff	Existing location Existing staff

None of these options represents a 'perfect solution' and we should recognise that is extremely unusual for an organisation to have total choice in how a call centre is established. Often pressures on existing premises means that new locations are required, and if these are located away from the existing business base, then new staff will almost certainly be necessary. By contrast, however, there may be a requirement to find roles for existing staff to avoid, or at least minimise, the need for possible redundancies. A further dilemma exists in the contrast between new staff, who may be more receptive to fresh ideas and working practices, compared with existing employees who may be 'set in their ways', yet have valuable knowledge concerning products and customers.

Most call centres will have been established following a series of compromises, and it is important to understand this process when determining structure and working practices.

Establishing the management structure

The establishment of a call centre is frequently seen as a 'new beginning' and the opportunity to challenge and change existing working practices. This situation may not be as straightforward as it first appears, but a popular area for change is in relation to structure and way the call centre operates. There is a consistent emphasis upon flatter structures, motivated by:

- improvements in the flow of communications;

- the development of a more democratic style of leadership;

- opportunities to reduce costs by reducing the layers of management.

These goals may be under threat, however, if the call centre is established around existing employees and working practices. Frequently, in such circumstances, an informal infrastructure will be in place, which may need to be challenged in the development of a new formal arrangement.

Most call centres have a structure based around 'agents', 'team leaders' (or supervisors) and 'centre managers'. The size of the operation, in terms of headcount, the complexity of the services offered and whether or not the operation is 24 hours, will all impact upon the optimum approach to management structure in relation to how working relationships are defined. Subject to these variations, around ten agents would normally be overseen by a team leader, with up to five team leaders reporting to a manager. This basic structure may be augmented by some of the following specialist roles:

- training;

- human resources;

- process improvement;

- performance management;

- IT.

What is important is that, in the evolution from previous working arrangements, the temptation to preserve 'casual' management relationships is avoided. A structure, reflecting the operational needs of the centre should be established, and this is the arrangement that should prevail, rather than any compromise based upon inherited circumstances.

There is a consistent theme, when new call centres are established, towards slimmer and simpler management structures. In the UK, while this more streamlined approach is achieved in many cases, the traditional hierarchies of 'management' and 'staff' are preserved.

Flexible working

Every call centre should be structured to achieve the organisation's business objectives, strategies and operational requirements. There will be similarities that allow us to identify common trends and themes, but operational differences can be vast. This is particularly true when establishing a working pattern that reflects the needs of the business. Call centres had their origins when the travel and hospitality industries began to centralise their reservation booking systems in the early 1970s. At virtually the same time companies began to awaken to the commercial possibilities of offering their goods and services to customers at times outside of the standard working day. When other organisations such as companies selling products through catalogues and financial services institutions began to see the possibilities that call centres afforded, a new type of operation began to emerge.

Probably less than 25% of current call centres are open 24 hours, but they have nevertheless presented a radical challenge to the '9 to 5', Monday to Friday, 'typical working week'. Organisations require call centres to be available to respond to customer demand, and a significant challenge in the development of appropriate contractual relationships has been to minimise, and where possible eliminate, the payment of premium rates of pay for working outside the traditional working day. This is another area where the balance between customer service and cost containment is a sensitive one, and if the demands for contractual flexibility are too great, this may ultimately have an adverse effect upon service levels.

There are four major types of employment contract currently in operation within the UK.

Agreed hours

This will specify the number of hours worked per week, and a pre-determined start and finish time. This is closest to the traditional form of contract and may well specify 0900–1700 working. Equally, however, it could be 1000–1800 or a reduced (i.e. part-time) work pattern.

Flexible hours

This will also have a specific number of hours per week, but to be worked within agreed parameters, such as 0800 to 2000, Monday to Saturday. This arrangement provides managers with greater flexibility to respond to the peaks and troughs of demand, but is likely to be less popular with staff, particularly if there are dramatic fluctuations in the pattern required on a week-to-week basis.

Annual hours

Such systems organise employees' working time on the basis of a number of hours over a year rather than a week. They often incorporate a 'banking' element so that in periods of low activity 'debit' time is accumulated as fewer hours are worked. Conversely, 'credit' time is built up when demand is high, and the principal idea behind annualisation is that debit and credit time will cancel out over the course of the year. Such a system can carry advantages both for employer and employee, but it may be costly to establish and administer.

Zero hours

Under this arrangement there is no set number of hours agreed, and the required pattern is established weekly or monthly as appropriate. This can potentially be a mutually convenient arrangement for both employer and employee. It suits in particular those where domestic circumstances do not allow a commitment to a regular pattern of working, while providing managers with the opportunity to call upon experienced additional resources when the need arises. There may, however, be an issue if notice is required on the part of the employee while the need of the manager is an immediate one.

Most call centres have the technology to monitor the pattern of calls taking place, whether incoming or outbound, and this provides the opportunity to determine appropriate staffing levels to reflect demand. In the early stages of call centre development, this demand was focused around the traditional working day, and financial services institutions, for example, experienced little demand for bill paying services in the early hours of the morning. Now customers are becoming more used to this greater availability and are increasingly seeking to avoid traditional peak times. Additionally more and more institutions are marketing their services globally via the Internet, and this means that 24-hour availability becomes essential.

A number of American IT companies have experienced problems in recruiting technically qualified help-desk staff to work 'unsocial hours'. Their radical solution has been the establishment of a series of call centres across different time zones. Thus, whatever geographical location the customer is calling from, at whatever time of day, the call can be routed to a location where the time is 'normal'.

While such solutions will not be available to all, a well-run call centre must have the capacity to respond to the peaks and troughs of customer demand. In general terms, the more hours the call centre is open, the more likely it is to take advantage of staff working less than full-time hours. This can carry certain advantages for both employer and employee:

- Employee turnover tends to be lower among part-time staff.

- If the organisation's policies are perceived as 'family-friendly', this can have a positive impact upon morale.

- If the work is, of necessity, repetitive or routine then shorter exposure time is likely to maintain service levels.

By contrast, there can be some negative elements:

- Domestic circumstances may not always permit the degree of flexibility that changes in customer demand require.

- The administrative implications of different contractual relationships and working patterns can be extremely time consuming for managers and team leaders.

- High numbers of part-time staff can lead to an increase in training costs.

The challenge is to ensure that well trained and motivated employees are available to respond to customer needs, at the appropriate times, and at a cost consistent with the overall business strategy.

Performance management

The statement concerning well-trained and motivated staff may seem an obvious one, and yet research shows that some 50% of people leaving a call centre environment do so because they found the work monotonous and unchallenging.

Organisations have found the advantages offered by call centres in improving business efficiency and making themselves available to customers at 'non-traditional times' to be highly persuasive. What appears to have happened, on numerous occasions, however, is that this quest has been accompanied by a failure to appreciate the basic principles of effective management. In an effective call centre a process is established to ensure that agents receive feedback and, as a result of this, motivation from positive and successful dealings with their customers. Provided this is supported by management placing equal emphasis on quality and quantity, then the building blocks are in place for a positive working environment.

By contrast, if insufficient attention is paid to the nature of the work, then life for a call centre employee can be regimented and frustrating. If there is little or no opportunity to demonstrate initiative or have some control over work processes, then this will inevitably lead to demotivated employees who will ultimately leave. Virtually everyone is seeking good working conditions, varied work and a sense of belonging in their job role. Call centre agents are no different in this respect, but the emphasis upon technology and measurement has sometimes led employers to ignore these basic requirements.

Effective performance management means that agents have a clear understanding of what their job entails and the standards against which they are to be measured. It also requires effective review and feedback mechanisms to ensure that they understand that progress is being made. Finally it requires the means by which training and coaching needs can be identified and put into action.

Once again, these basic principles are as important to the agents in a call centre environment as elsewhere.

The three main elements to the performance management process are the *job description* (or profile), the *review* (or appraisal) and the *personal development plan*. These should be linked to the delivery of an appropriate reward structure:

Job description

The type of work at the centre will influence the precise content of the job description. Does it deal with inbound or outbound calls, or both? Is there a sales role required or rather the provision of customer information? The core should, however, contain most of the following:

- *Purpose of the role.* This provides, in one or two sentences, the key elements required in the position.

- *Primary accountabilities.* This lists the various parts that make up the job as a whole. The sentences should contain descriptive verbs, such as 'plan', 'provide', 'participate', 'write' or 'respond'.

- *Key result areas/performance standards for the role.* This identifies the standards against which effective job performance is evaluated. It is likely that measures of customer service will feature significantly, but profit maximisation and cost reduction are also likely to be relevant. The degree of technical sophistication in the vast majority of call centres provides the opportunity for a variety of statistics and performance measures to be generated around response times, call duration times, overall numbers of customers spoken to, number of queries resolved/sales achieved, etc. Such information should be used carefully, as we will discuss in greater detail later.

• *Qualifications/experience required for the role.* This will establish what is necessary in terms of academic qualifications, levels of computer literacy and relevant work experience, either in terms of the industry in question or, more broadly, exposure to customer contact in previous jobs.

Competencies

If competencies have been developed for the role, they should also appear in the job description. What, however, is of fundamental importance is that the document is 'live' rather than an academic exercise with no relevance to day-to-day work activity. On far too many occasions energy and effort has been expended in creating a job description when a role is new or advertising is required. On completion, the document is then consigned to the files until further recruits are required.

This is a frustrating waste of the time spent in preparing the description, which can be a highly relevant reference document. The best way to overcome such problems is to make it clear that ownership of the content of the form is the responsibility of the job holder. In this way they can be encouraged to ensure its content is always relevant and up to date, and this can then be the basis of the performance review or appraisal, which can then be carried out with a very clear understanding of the requirements of the role.

Performance review

Without question, it is this element of the performance management process that has attracted the greatest attention in terms of training, articles, books and commentaries. There has been a bewildering variety of suggestions and ideas in respect of form design, evaluation categories and scoring mechanisms. It is not within the scope of this book to comment in detail on these alternatives. Indeed, it can be argued that placing too great an emphasis on such matters can obscure the primary reason for the review. This should offer the employee and the manager the opportunity to discuss, on a regular basis, the effectiveness of past work performance and what is required to maintain or improve this in the future.

In most organisations a tradition has developed where the review or appraisal has taken place annually. Developments in call centres have tended to move away from this tradition to a series of interim reviews, frequently on a quarterly basis and in some cases more often. This is a development we welcome and would recommend a quarterly review cycle as representing best practice.

There is evidence to suggest that on numerous occasions, the pressurised nature of the call centre environment has meant that effective performance review has been absent. It is, however, as important in the context of a call centre as any other and if difficulties surrounding the repetitious nature of many call centre activities are to be overcome, the review process and its relationship to the personal development plan is vital.

Personal development plan

The purpose of the plan is to identify areas of training and coaching, which will either improve or add to the skills, knowledge and experience of the job holder. It will also identify the timescales in which these changes will take place and the measures against which they will be compared. An effective personal development plan should include:

- *Development area.* This defines the subject of the development activity such as handling difficult customers, improving product knowledge or learning a new computer application.

- *What outcome do I want?* This describes the goal to be attained.

- *What will I do?* Will training away from the job be required, or in conjunction with work colleagues?

- *What support do I need?* This may be described in terms of resources or time away from the normal job role.

- *How do I describe success?* What measures will be applied to my new skills?

- *When will this happen?* This defines the timescales to be worked towards.

The key message is that the call centre environment does not require the work that has been dedicated to performance management in the past to be rewritten. Many of the techniques and methods that have evolved in organisations can be adapted successfully. Indeed there is a danger that the very fact that call centres are a relatively recent development encourages fundamental changes to the way people are managed and motivated. The 'dark satanic mills' argument is a direct result of technological and processing considerations taking precedence over the needs of those working within them.

The organisation of work

Given the diversity of products, services and information now dealt with within call centres, it is impossible to provide a single model that defines the organisation of work. It is important, however, to keep in mind that the evolution of call centres combined a number of interrelated goals:

- the exploitation of new technology;

- the opportunity to obtain economies of scale and efficiencies by dealing with customers on a more centralised basis;

- the opportunity to develop customer relationships, and to provide feedback to the rest of the business with greater levels of sophistication than had previously been possible.

To achieve these ambitions people working in call centres need to be skilled in dealing with customer demands and expectations, and have the necessary levels of knowledge and experience to respond accordingly. If work is organised in such a way that it is dull, repetitive and uninspiring, then these goals will not be achieved.

This is not to deny the existence of routine tasks – in fact the very basis of the call centre concept implies that this will be a factor. What is crucial is that this is recognised and appropriate action taken to address its implications.

Retention

Employee retention has been identified as an area of concern in call centres, and research into reasons for leaving has provided evidence that pay issues are far from the major reason for departure. Just as likely to be mentioned are problems such as:

- the nature of the work itself;

- the lack of opportunities for advancement;

- the failure to provide appropriate training;

- a lack of clarity in relation to career paths;

- relationships with team leaders or colleagues.

Introducing different supervisory levels into the structure of a call centre can be used to motivate employees with the prospect of promotion. It should also be recognised, however, that many individuals working within this type of environment are not seeking additional responsibility. There is also a danger that promoting agents who demonstrate effective customer relationship skills may be counter-productive if they are ill prepared for the requirements of a supervisor's role.

Introducing variety into the tasks employees carry out means that they are able to develop new skills and can relieve the more monotonous elements of the job. Additional responsibility need not mean that a supervisory element is introduced. In one newly established call centre familiar to the authors, the employees, at an early stage of their employment with the company, were encouraged to identify an additional area of responsibility they would like to be involved with. They were able to choose from some of the following:

• participation in future recruitment activity;

• involvement with induction and/or product knowledge training.

• involvement with the design and development of incentive programmes;

• evaluating the effectiveness of existing work methods and procedures.

To ensure the success of such a programme requires a commitment on the part of the employer that people will be entitled to spend some of their working time away from direct contact with the customer.

Such an approach carries some additional costs, but these will be more than outweighed by the retention of experienced and knowledgeable people with a greater understanding of the needs of the business. It will also contribute to the making of successful and better informed decisions about the key areas of activity described above.

Designing the most appropriate reward structure

The evolution of the call centre industry in the UK has resulted in a concentration of sites in certain geographical locations. Regions that were originally perceived as 'low cost' were chosen as the technology utilised meant that close proximity to the customers was no longer a primary consideration.

However, the explosive growth of the sector has meant a degree of saturation has been reached in a number of locations. This has meant that employers must increasingly turn to new methods of attracting and retaining people in order to maintain an effective workforce.

As before, it remains true that call centres should be aware of – and learn – the lessons of more traditional industries when devising reward structures appropriate to their needs.

Basic pay

Basic pay remains the key component of any reward package, and how it is determined will depend on the extent to which the organisation has already established structures. Geography and the mix of people between the new and the established, the less experienced and the more experienced, will influence the ability to introduce new arrangements. Increasingly, however, employers are seeking to provide rewards in ways other than through basic pay. There are two principle reasons for this:

- In call centres, the trend is to link reward to performance. Basic pay is seen as inflexible when there is a desire to reward superior performance or additional effort. In such circumstances making a bonus an increasingly important element of the overall reward package is considered attractive.

- In locations where the concentration of call centres is high, some element of 'trading up' basic salaries has already taken place, as experienced agents recognise they are a scarce resource and thus have gained bargaining power. Employers are now recognising the need to break away from this potentially dangerous upward spiral by placing greater emphasis on other elements of the package.

Bonus

There is the potential to base bonus payments on four major elements of performance:

- the performance (usually the profitability) of the company as a whole;

- the performance of the call centre itself;

- the results of the various teams which constitute the centre;

- individual performance.

To complicate matters further, various combinations of these options are also possible, for example team-based rewards supplemented by the incentive of a year-end bonus based on overall company performance.

Bonus as a motivator

What is clear, however, is that bonus as a motivational tool is most effective when an individual can perceive a clear relationship between their own performance and the level of bonus paid.

This may appear an obvious statement, but an analysis of the evolution of bonus philosophy can assist us. We have already seen that the desire to move away from total reliance on basic pay has been around for some time. This trend established itself in the sales sector, and thus positions within estate agency, for example, have a long tradition of basing a significant element of reward on commission or bonus arrangements.

More recently this trend has developed further throughout the financial services and retail sectors, but it remains true that it has been primarily associated with sales roles. This is because the existence of targets and specific measures of performance in relation to 'units' sold make the design and implementation of bonus-based schemes relatively straightforward.

The challenge has been to replicate these ideas in jobs where the major part of the work is administration, customer service or processing. In these areas the 'hard numbers' are much less easy to define. Despite attempts to base payment systems on the attainment of individual objectives, there is often a strong element of subjectivity, and thus schemes based on the overall performance of the call centre or company have proved popular, in effect as a compromise.

Sales are a key element in the life of many call centres, and where this is the case, schemes based at team or individual level are frequently in place. Additionally, the use of technology to record, monitor and evaluate many of the activities that take place leads to the potential to measure clerical and administrative tasks as never before.

Call waiting times, abandonment rates, the duration of calls and a variety of other measures, coupled with the ability of supervisors to monitor conversations between agents and customers, have brought us much closer to objective measurement for non-sales roles. This has not been without its problems, however, and much of the adverse publicity call centres have attracted has been a consequence of the inappropriate usage of such measurements. This issue persists in some locations, but managers and HR staff are increasingly seeking to strike a balance between the setting of targets and goals, and the rewards that follow for their achievement.

Alternative methods of bonus payment

Measure	Pros	Cons
Company performance	Encourages ownership of overall company results	Too detached from local performance to be a meaningful incentive
Centre performance	Focuses on key goals and encourages flexibility in the range of tasks performed	Does not reflect the reality that variation in levels of success will exist

Team performance	Highly effective in creating the right spirit and focus on the task	Effective performers may feel they are 'carrying' some of the team members
Individual performance	Ensures that the greatest rewards go to those making the highest contribution	Can be divisive and discourage cooperation and flexibility

Other types of incentive

Motivated by the potentially monotonous nature of some elements of call centre activity, increased attention has been devoted to looking for alternative methods of rewarding staff, while maintaining a sense of fun and enjoyment within the workplace. These can vary greatly in their scope and cost, from lavish holidays to a modest gift presented at the desk.

Often such initiatives are centred on the team and the authors have encountered incentives based upon areas as diverse as:

*   horse racing (the Grand National);

*   the Monopoly board game;

*   a Las Vegas casino;

- Green Shield stamps!

The list is potentially endless, as are the rewards linked to success. Non-financial incentives are often perceived as maintaining a sense of fun, while ensuring that recognition becomes memorable and positive.

As with any reward scheme, the ability to respond to the areas that motivate a particular individual is a key consideration. A number of specialist organisations now offer 'experiences' which range from the daredevil to the indulgent. The opportunity to offer a successful employee the opportunity to participate in the 'once in a lifetime' opportunity of white-water rafting or motor racing can be balanced with a night at the theatre or a restaurant meal for those of a more sedate frame of mind.

Such activities combine the memorable with that vital element of personal choice, but external assistance is not necessary for an effective incentive programme. Schemes that provide the opportunity for additional time off – from a modest addition to the lunch break to additional days annual leave – can prove very popular. Similarly in some locations the allocation of a prime car parking space to the 'Employee of the Month' can be highly prized. In response to the question, 'What is the most memorable incentive you have awarded?', a manager assisting our research replied, 'a jar of pickled onions!'

Space does not permit a detailed explanation of the circumstances that led up to this somewhat unusual award. It reminds us, however, that call centres have introduced radical changes to the organisation of work. The key to ensuring that working practices, performance management issues and appropriate reward systems work together towards the achievement of organisational goals lies in the effective combination of tried and tested techniques, coupled with an eye for innovation and sometimes the unusual.

Checklist of key actions

- There will rarely be a 'free hand' in determining the structure of a call centre, even if it is a newly established operation. Recognise this constraint, but look for every opportunity to introduce fresh concepts and new ideas.

- Keep the management structure simple. Effective communication is the key to success in a call centre environment. This is as relevant for teams, supervisors and managers as it is for customers.

- Be very clear how the pattern of working hours is to be supported. A plethora of different contractual types and shift patterns can become extremely cumbersome to administer.

- Agents in a call centre are not unique workers so do not treat them as if they are. The basic principles of performance management are the bedrock of an effective customer-orientated culture.

- Look for opportunities to introduce diversity into all job roles. Restricting opportunities for agents to learn new skills and experience new challenges will ultimately be counter-productive as problems with retention begin to appear.

- As with any working environment, a call centre will contain people whose motivation to work, and the rewards they are seeking, will differ. Recognise this diversity, and be flexible in how success is celebrated and rewarded.

CHAPTER 3

Getting the right people in place

Understanding the job requirements

Call centres are one of the fastest growing providers of job opportunities in the UK, and this growth shows no signs of slowing. In the early stages of their development, regions that were perceived to offer staff availability, often at lower costs than traditional operations, were targeted as desirable locations. Such has been the rate of growth, however, that some 50% of employers with call centre operations now report problems in terms of recruitment.

If there was ever a time when there was a 'ready market' from which to recruit, such a situation is rapidly disappearing. Against this background the need for an effective recruitment strategy is paramount. Despite the diversity of the services offered by call centres, when asked which attributes are most often found in successful call centre agents, managers are consistent in their responses. Not surprisingly, a dedication to customer service is pre-eminent.

Characteristics of successful call centre agents

- Strong customer service experience.

- Sales experience.

- Calm approach under pressure.

- A sense of humour.

- Patience.

- Willing and eager to learn.

- Ability to analyse facts and data.

- Diligent.

- Willingness to work with items of a repetitive nature.

- Ability to work effectively as part of a team.

- Keen to challenge traditional methods and procedures.

Another, perhaps more surprising, frequently heard comment was that previous call centre experience was not important.

Given the high rates of turnover experienced in some call centres, this may reflect a belief that the wrong types of recruits have been targeted in the past. Alternatively, it may reflect a desire to avoid importing the culture and potential 'bad habits' from another company.

For many outside the industry, the ideal call centre agent is seen as an extrovert, with an outgoing nature and 'bubbly' personality. In many quarters this is now being challenged, and there is recognition that work requiring attention to detail, the ability to learn swiftly and feel comfortable with technology may be better suited to a more introverted character. If the industry is to be successful in addressing the issues of recruitment and retention, then avoiding the placing of 'square pegs in round holes' must be a key priority!

Understanding the needs of new recruits

Because of the retention problems experienced by many call centres, research has looked to define key characteristics that influence the job or career outlook of agents. A variety of names have been assigned to these groups, but they can be characterised as follows:

- those seeking a long-term career and who will therefore value training and promotional opportunities highly;

- those who are job-mobile, perhaps content with a short-term contractual relationship, and keen on pay and training opportunities;

- those who require stable employment, and are seeking to be led rather than be leaders;

- those whose financial needs are paramount, and thus demonstrate a willingness to respond to incentives and rewards.

Virtually all call centres will be of sufficient size, in headcount terms, to display a mixture of people displaying all these characteristics. What is vital, in recruitment terms, is not which type may be superior or inferior job performers, but rather that by addressing particular needs, effort can be effectively targeted and thus results improved.

Developing the recruitment strategy

There is no single 'best practice' solution to call centre recruitment. Prior to embarking on a recruitment campaign it is essential to have a clear understanding of the issues and constraints that will influence the approach. Different issues and priorities will emerge in different circumstances, and a checklist like that provided below will ensure that all relevant factors are taken into account.

Checklist: key questions for defining the recruitment strategy

- Is the location a greenfield site or an existing location?

- Will the workforce be newly recruited, staff already employed or a mixture of both?

- What pattern of hours will agents be required to work in the new call centre. Is the call centre to be a 24-hour operation?

- Is there a specific requirement for knowledge, understanding or experience of a particular industry, product or system?

- What are the timescales before the call centre becomes operational?

- Are recruitment resources available, or is there a need to 'recruit and train the recruiters'?

- Will recruitment requirements be phased over a period of time (if so, how long?) or is the full headcount required on day 1?

- What is the size of the recruitment budget?

- What is the company philosophy on the use of external agents to handle some (or perhaps all) of the recruitment activity?

- What estimates are there of recruitment needs going forward?

- What will be the role of operational management in the recruitment process?

- What are the characteristics of the local labour market?

- What is the competition like for recruits?

- What monitoring processes will be in place to assess the suitability of new hires, post-recruitment?

- Is there a 'quota' regarding recruiting from one single company?

- Will there be a trial period or pilot operation?

- What plans are being made for induction training?

With the answers to these questions, the recruitment strategy can be developed both to support the overall business objectives, and also to assist in their definition.

If, for example, it is identified that the local recruitment market is highly competitive, a potential solution might be to attract candidates such as students or the older worker. Some groups may be unable, or unwilling, to work during the traditional 'core time' of 0900–1700. Do more flexible working practices fit the needs of the business? If initially the answer is no, can these be adapted, thus providing greater flexibility with recruitment options?

A number of organisations are now actively recruiting the over-40s. They argue that on top of offering additional recruitment opportunities, such a strategy also has the advantage of introducing experience and maturity into the workforce. If such an approach is to be adopted, it is important that its implications are considered in the development of recruitment strategies. Older workers can often assume that positions are destined for younger people, and this perception may be reinforced if the nature of the recruitment advertising is developed with young candidates in mind. The wording and graphics of such advertising should be carefully considered to ensure it does not, perhaps inadvertently, exclude some categories of potential applicants.

Recruitment and selection procedures: some alternatives

The interview

There has been much justifiable criticism of the interview being a subjective selection device when used in isolation from other forms of assessment. However, it remains a vital tool which is difficult to imagine discarding, and when used correctly it can be effective. The call centre environment is well suited to making effective use of its advantages. We have seen that the key attribute required by an agent is the ability to provide exemplary customer service, and the interview can assist in determining if this characteristic is in evidence.

Problems with traditional interviews

Research into the effectiveness of traditional interviews has found them to be inadequate in a number of ways. Studies have found that unstructured selection interviews have little power to predict who will do a good job.

Standard interview questions such as *'What are your strengths and weaknesses?'* and *'What jobs have you liked and not liked?'* are less than effective for the following reasons:

- Generally people do not have any real understanding of their strengths and weaknesses.

- Even if they do they are unlikely to want to share anything about their weaknesses during a recruitment interview.

- People are frequently reluctant to reveal their true motives during an interview.

- During interviews people answer in the way they perceive the interviewer wants them to respond.

Competency-based interviews

The use of competency-based interviews is becoming increasingly popular in a wide range of organisations, including call centres, as they can deliver a higher degree of objectivity in the selection process. Because they are based on proven job requirements, they are found to be more effective in recruiting people who are more likely to be suited to the job more quickly.

Once a set of competencies has been developed for a job, candidates can be tested, during the interview, for how well they demonstrate these competencies. This can be done by adopting a planned and structured approach to questioning and by being aware of the competencies that are required for doing the job successfully. Not only does this result in more effective interviewing it also considerably increases the level of objectivity applied in the interview. This is achieved by ensuring that each candidate is asked the same range of questions and are assessed on the same criteria.

Competency-based job profiles and descriptions

The starting point in approaching an interview from the perspective of competencies is the preparation of a competency-based job profile. It is constructed by reviewing those competencies that are identified as being most important for each job. Competencies can be defined as being *those things a person needs to be good at if they are to be good at their job*. Preparing a job profile means listing all the tasks and activities of a job and then identifying the most important.

In an average job this should work out as being no more than six to ten critical competencies, in other words the six to ten things the job holder needs to be good at. Many jobs will, of course, have less than ten critical competencies but this can only be decided when conducting a review of the job.

In the example below we have identified six critical competencies for a call centre agent. Identifying the tasks and activities in this way will enable you to identify the sort of person you are looking for. Including an indication of the key result areas and accountabilities, as described in the previous chapter under job descriptions, can further develop the profile.

Examples of competencies for call centre agents, with supporting interview questions

Customer focus

- 'Tell me about your most challenging customer, and how you handled the situation.'

- 'Give me an example of when you gave a customer exemplary service.'

Teamworking

- 'How would you describe the most successful team that you have been a member of?'

- 'What experience do you have of helping to coach other people to learn new skills?'

Persuading

- 'How do you approach persuading people to a particular point of view?'

- 'Give me an example of an occasion when you have successfully persuaded someone to change their point of view.'

Problem solving

- 'Describe an occasion when you were able to generate an innovative solution to a problem.'

- 'What is the most frustrating aspect of your current role? How would you like to change it?'

Results orientation

- 'Tell me about the most challenging deadline you have faced, and how you responded to it.'

- 'How is your performance assessed in your current role?'

Self-development

- 'How do you respond when you receive criticism from someone else?'

- 'Give me an example of an activity you have undertaken, to assist your development, in the last six months.'

An interview assessment form should be completed immediately after the interview, to help assess the candidate against the competencies. A sample form based on the above competencies is shown on the following pages.

Post-Interview Assessment Form

Appointment of:

Name of candidate:

Date of interview:

As part of your preparation for this set of interviews you will have identified the competencies that are essential for success in this position. Note these below and use them to help focus your assessment of each candidate. (You should assess the candidate on a scale of 1 = poor, not acceptable; 6 = outstanding, very acceptable.)

Competence to be assessed	Score	Additional comments
1 Customer focus		
2 Teamworking		
3 Persuading		
4 Problem solving		
5 Results orientation		
6 Self-development		
Total score		

Other criteria to be assessed:

Educational background:

Previous work experience:

Overall assessment:

Think about the candidate and how you assess their ability to fill the position you are interviewing for. Write your comments below and award an overall score as you did for each competency.

_____

_____

_____

_____

The telephone interview

Given that all call centre agents will spend a substantial part of their work time using the telephone, it is surprising that the telephone interview is not more effectively employed in the recruitment process. While not a replacement for the face-to-face interview, it has the potential to add value to the selection process by providing a more detailed and objective viewpoint. Added to this is the potential for time to be saved by identifying inappropriate applicants at an early stage of the process.

Recruitment advertising can only supply a limited amount of information to potential candidates. Any interview is a two-way exchange of information, and effective use of the telephone provides the opportunity both to clarify areas of uncertainty, while at the same time ensuring that the applicant is clear on the requirements of the position. Thus initial contact can be used to:

- clarify any aspects of the application form or CV which have either been omitted or are unclear;

- gain an understanding of salary expectations;

- provide information in relation to work patterns, particularly if there is a requirement for shift, weekend or other activity involving 'non-standard' arrangements;

- expand the information supplied in advertising concerning terms, conditions and benefits.

This last point can be particularly helpful if there is a need, in a competitive recruitment market, to 'sell' the advantages of the organisation.

Having established common ground (or otherwise) in the areas described above, the telephone can also be used to ask similar questions linked to job competencies, as has already been suggested. Vitally, however, there is also the opportunity to assess the effectiveness of the applicant in relation to their telephone technique.

A scale, assessing use of English and tone of voice, can be devised as shown on the next page.

While this does not completely eradicate the element of subjectivity, by combining this assessment with the response to interview questions and job information, a detailed picture of the candidate begins to emerge.

We recommend that telephone interviews become a standard part of the recruitment process for call centres. They must, however, be an integral part of that process, and certain key elements must be borne in mind:

Assessment of telephone technique

0   Aggressive, negative style / use of offensive language.

1   Difficult to understand or overbearing in manner / use of slang expressions.

2   Mumbles or pronounced mannerisms / poor vocabulary / interruptions or over-long pauses.

3   Non-assertive / speech lacks appropriate pace and intonation.

4   Rhythm, speed, volume, pitch (RSVP).

5   Good vocabulary / calm and confident / asks questions to clarify.

6   Highly professional image / articulate and confident / positive and warm.

- Remember the law. During a telephone interview you must not say or ask anything that would not be a part of a face-to-face interview.

- Suit the questions to the role. A potential team leader should, for example, be quizzed concerning their experience of leading, motivating and coaching others.

- Research shows that the majority of candidates would prefer to participate in a telephone interview in the early evening. Does your present operation have suitably qualified staff available at this time?

- Used properly, telephone interviews can be an effective and efficient way to use time, contain costs and potentially lay the foundation for better employee retention.

Assessment centres

An assessment centre provides an opportunity to expose job applicants to a range of selection methods, in addition to the interview. Among the most popular are exercises designed to evaluate teamworking and role-plays of different sorts of customer calls. They also provide the opportunity to administer a variety of psychometric and ability tests.

Assessment centres provide additional rigour and objectivity to the selection process, but they are demanding in terms of the time and people resource required to make them effective. In researching this book the authors encountered a number of organisations that had established assessment centres to recruit for newly created call centres. In the main they were found to be inappropriate to cope with the ongoing demands of providing new recruits to a 'live' and active operation, except in the larger call centres where there is significant ongoing demand for recruitment.

Before devoting time and resources to the development of an assessment centre approach, organisations need to be confident that such methods are sustainable in the reality of a competitive marketplace.

Testing

The range of tests now available to support the recruitment and selection process is increasingly diverse. They can be categorised into a number of broad headings:

- *Ability tests* – these can assess numeric skills or verbal reasoning ability. In addition, this category would also include assessments of keyboard skills and speed of data input.

- *Psychometric tests* – these attempt to identity the personality or potential of the candidate. They may focus either on the individual or their potential contribution to the work of a team.

- *Simulations* – these are a more recent development, and through the use of PC-based technology create 'real life scenarios to expose applicants to the range of call centre activities. At a basic level they test for the accuracy of audio data entry skills, but can also involve a more in-depth evaluation that requires candidates to respond to different customer requests and options of screen choice.

The two major principles to be followed in the effective utilisation of tests are:

- Ensure that they are an integral part of the recruitment process. Some tests can be both time-consuming and labour-intensive, particularly if administered to individual candidates. Assessment centres can be a useful way of testing a range of candidates effectively and efficiently.

- Be very clear about what is being sought. This can be relatively easy to define in relation to data entry, numeric ability and the like, but more difficult in relation to personality. We have commented earlier in this book that the perceived view of the characteristics of a successful agent is under challenge. A key element of the process is to compare the results of tests to agent performance. This will ensure that they have a real contribution to make to the recruitment process.

Internal recruitment

Problems with attracting the right candidates and dealing with retention issues have meant that external recruitment has been one of the main challenges for call centre operations. Often ignored, however, is the process by which supervisors and team leaders are chosen. There is a natural propensity to reward the best performing agents with promotional opportunities. The skills and personality which make someone suited to be an effective team member are often not those that are required for someone who supervises the work.

Because of this the methods of supervisor selection merit careful consideration. In these circumstances the assessment centre approach may be highly desirable, as internal candidates provide greater flexibility in terms of availability and there is ready access to existing information about their performance.

In using assessment centres for internal appointments it is essential to handle carefully the question of feedback to the unsuccessful candidates and to have in place a strategy for re-entry.

Exit interviews

In addition to taking care with recruitment we strongly recommend that a strategy for assessing why people leave is in place and used.

Assessing and tracking why people leave is an essential element in enabling the HR process to make a full contribution to organisational success.

Checklist of key actions

- Avoid making assumptions about the experience and personality of potential recruits. Over 50% of leavers from call centres state they have no desire to work in one again.

- A range of different factors should determine the recruitment strategy. The essential requirement is that there is a strategy, rather than an ad-hoc response to unforeseen complications.

- Look for opportunities to gather as much information as possible about potential recruits, but remember that the recruitment process has to match the operational needs of the business.

- The telephone is the 'tool of the trade' in a call centre. It makes sense, therefore, to use it as an element in recruitment.

- Develop key competencies for agents and use them to assess the suitability of candidates during recruitment.

- Pay particular attention to the internal methods of selecting supervisors and team leaders. Successful candidates will swiftly need to adapt to a very different style of working. Mistakes can be costly in terms of their impact upon morale and productivity.

- Create a role for agents in the recruitment and selection of new members of the team. They can contribute valuable insights, and will relish the opportunity to make such a contribution.

- Establish a process for gathering information about why people leave.

CHAPTER 4

Training and development

There is an increasing recognition within all organisations that if they are to be able to compete effectively in our knowledge-based economy they need to employ people who are highly skilled, knowledgeable and motivated. Nowhere is this more true than within call centres. Employees, however, are only one part of the people element in organisational success, the other one being customers.

For many customers the only part of an organisation they come into contact with is a call centre. This makes it even more important to ensure that call centre agents are committed to their own success and the success of their organisation.

Key questions for a call centre manager are:

- What do call centre agents need to be good at if they are to be effective at their job?

- How can this knowledge, skill, attitude and motivation be developed?

It is possible to start answering such questions through a training needs analysis.

Analysing training needs

Any analysis of training needs should look at training requirement from two perspectives:

- *The needs of the organisation* – what are the really important skills, knowledge and attitudes required of the people doing a particular job? Knowing this can help to focus attention on the training needs of a group of people.

- *The needs of individual employees* – what particular skills knowledge and attitude does each individual need to develop to bring him or her up to the standard required for the job? Being able to answer this enables the manger to identify individual training needs.

The first of these is the essential starting point for any call centre manager who wants to ensure they have a clear understanding of what an agent needs to be good at if they are to be good at their job. Without this understanding it is difficult:

- to identify the competencies required for effective performance;

- to set standards of performance;

- to set standards for recruitment;

- to develop plans for training.

The specific elements of the training plan should be developed within the context of each call centre. This is best done by conducting some simple research to identify the knowledge, skills and attitude most likely to contribute to an individual being a successful agent. The research can be conducted by:

- observing agents when they are working in order to identify the application of which behaviours contribute to success;

- talking to call centre managers and team leaders;

- visiting call centres to increase your own knowledge and understanding of what success looks like;

- reading extensively publications which can shed light on what behaviours contribute to success in a call centre.

We referred earlier in this book to the value that call centre managers can gain from benchmarking. Benchmarking the competencies for agents can help to shed light on what it is that agents need to be good at.

Once the information has been collected, whether through benchmarking or informally, it should be possible to develop a role profile identifying the personal attributes and behaviours most likely to contribute to success. This profile can then be used as a basis for identifying competencies, setting standards of performance and developing plans for training.

Analysing the training needs of individual agents

The second step in the process is to measure existing or new agents against the defined competencies and standards. This can be done for new agents by making sure that the recruitment process is professional and geared to identifying people who already have some of the attributes you have identified as contributing to success.

For existing agents a process of observation and assessment will be required to identify what particular skills or behaviours each individual needs to develop if they are to improve performance. It is important to understand that performance improvement is a gradual, not an instant process. People are more likely to be successful if they develop and apply a small number of new skills rather than trying to develop all the skills required at the same time.

At the end of the book we have provided in an appendix an example of a form for assessing performance quality and identifying training needs.

Training

Notwithstanding the above, it is possible to identify some elements of training likely to apply in the majority of call centres and for the majority of agents. We have produced below the objectives and a brief description of four programmes we consider to be essential for any call centre. All of the programmes below are intended to be held away from the job but in the call centre location, with participants working in small groups or one to one. All training should be followed by the trainer or team leader observing the agent in action. The final step is for the trainer or team leader to provide feedback and coaching to the agent as necessary to build on and improve skills already developed.

All training should emphasise the practical rather than the theoretical, if the training does not consist of a minimum of 50% practical hands-on learning it is less likely to be effective.

Induction training

Too many organisations try to pretend that they can get away with providing only a minimum of induction training. This is a mistake and for a call centre can be a disaster. It is understandable that some managers take this view, as there is such pressure to get new agents operational as quickly as possible. It should, however, be resisted as time spent preparing a new agent is never wasted. The key is to make sure that everything done during the induction programme can be seen to contribute to the effectiveness of the agent once they start work. In some organisations a separate operational room is used where agents under training can work for some time handling live calls under close supervision. In such circumstances it is recognised that the trainee agent will learn best on the job, but in the early stage will require exceptional support.

Objectives

Upon completion of the training participants will:

* understand fully their role as a call centre agent;

* be aware of the objectives which will be set for them as a newly appointed agent;

- have developed the technical skills required for using the telephony installed in the call centre;

- have developed skills in the standard way of using the telephone and practised this;

- have practised and received feedback on how they handle customers when dealing with a range of typical queries;

- have been introduced to the company or organisation and be able to describe the role of the call centre in achieving the overall objectives of the business;

- have been introduced to the practical issues of working in the call centre and be able to describe key elements of the health and safety policy as they impact on the work of an agent;

- have completed an assessment of their learning and understand that unless they achieve the required pass mark in all subjects they will have to undertake the training again;

- have developed a personal training plan with clearly stated objectives covering their first six months of employment.

Description

Ideally induction training should take place in small groups but if necessary can take place on a one-to-one basis. It does not have to take place on successive days but can extend over a couple of weeks. The most appropriate structure should reflect the needs of the call centre and, of course, the trainees. If the programme is to be held over a week or a couple of weeks there is always a danger that pressure may be exerted to cut the programme short, but such pressure should be resisted.

If the skills of new employees have not been assessed at recruitment they should be assessed at the start of the induction programme. This way the emphasis of the programme can be adjusted to meet the needs of participants, although it should still cover all the objectives as stated.

Assessment at the end of the programme is also essential and this should lead to each participant writing a personal development plan for the first months of his or her employment. Following the completion of the programme this plan should be discussed with the team leader and activities agreed and scheduled to enable the skills identified to be developed.

Building customer contact skills

The relationship the agent is able to create with the customer, whether responding to or initiating a call, is a key element in the effectiveness of the agent. As the majority of agents only have a very short time to make an impression, their ability to build relationships quickly and easily on the telephone can make a real difference. We continue to be amazed that some organisations still fail to recognise that the skills, techniques, styles and approaches used by agents can have a significant impact on how they are perceived by the customer. If a relationship can be established the likelihood of the agent completing a successful call is greatly improved. We accept that some people have a natural style that allows them to create relationships more easily, but we also know that everyone can improve their skills in relationship building through training.

Objectives

Upon completion of the training participants will:

*   be equipped to build relationships with customers quickly and easily;

*   understand how to lead and control a conversation in a way that allows the customer to feel comfortable;

- be able to use their voice as a key tool in creating the right impression;

- have developed important skills in asking questions and listening;

- understand how to quickly get to the point of what the customer needs;

- be able to use a cycle of conversation enabling them to achieve a balance between giving and gathering information;

- be equipped to bring conversations to a satisfactory end;

- have practised and received feedback on each of the above skills.

Description

Every agent should attend such a programme once they have completed induction training and have become familiar with the basic skills of using the technology, product knowledge and dealing with customers over the telephone. The training should be carried out in small groups but if necessary can take place one to one. Small groups are better as the learning can be shared and participants can have some fun with role-plays and practice sessions. Further follow-up and refresher sessions should be attended as appropriate and can also introduce more developed skills and techniques.

All agents should be encouraged to understand that improvement is always possible and the provision of regular training is one way of reinforcing this view. As mentioned above the training should be supported, by further coaching on the job, after observation and assessment.

Getting the most out of the technology

It is easy to assume that once the induction programme has been completed the agents will be familiar and equipped to use the particular technology installed at the call centre. It is true that the induction programme should introduce the agents to the technology and equip them with basic skills. It is unlikely, however, that every agent can become fully proficient with all aspects of the technology at induction. Many call centres use technology which provides a number of options for the agent to offer alternatives and improve service. Some additional training may therefore be necessary.

The training should take place in small groups but if necessary can take place one to one. Small groups are better as the learning can be shared and participants can have some fun with role-plays and practice sessions.

It is not appropriate for us to describe this training in any detail as the content and relevance will depend entirely on the technology in use in a particular call centre.

Developing team leader skills

It is difficult to overstate the added value that effective team leaders can bring to a call centre. As in many other parts of an organisation the role of the team leader can be crucial to the running of a successful business unit. In a call centre, however, it can be argued that this role is even more important. It is widely agreed that the team leader can be pivotal in determining the success of a team in a call centre. Therefore the selection and training of this key group of people needs to be handled with care.

We mentioned in Chapter 2 that the best team leader may not necessarily be drawn from the best agents. Organisations that want to avoid the obvious problem of appointing an ineffective team leader and losing an effective agent need to break from the past when the only way of continuing to reward the best performer was to promote them. Such organisations should review their systems for reward and promotion. Having said that, of course, many good agents have the ability to become good team leaders.

What then of the skills required for an effective team leader? We can identify a number that are essential. Effective team leaders will be able to:

- inspire and motivate;

- communicate clearly and understandably;

- lead effective meetings;

- build winning teams;

- monitor and troubleshoot issues within the team;

- represent the team;

- deal with difficult customers;

- observe agents in action;

- assess the performance of agents;

- provide feedback to agents;

- coach agents in achieving improved performance;

- apply a flexible leadership style;

- cope with the pressure of the position.

This is not an exhaustive list and we are confident there will be more that a team leader needs to do. We believe, however, that if an individual does not have the capacity to achieve the above it is unlikely they will be effective as a team leader.

Prior to appointment team leaders should be expected to undergo a strenuous selection process. This process should allow call centre management to identify those people who they believe have the capacity to achieve the above. It is important to create a climate in which those not selected do not feel they have failed, and they must continue to be valued and rewarded for the contribution they make. Careful debriefing after the selection process can help but more helpful is to create over time a climate that enables people to apply for the position with the expectation that not everyone who applies will be accepted.

Training following appointment is essential. It is likely that many of those selected will already have many of the skills required, but they will need to refine and develop them and understand how to apply them. Ideally, in our view, the training for team leaders should take place in small groups either in or away from the call centre. We say this because it will be important not only to train team leaders but to build a team. We recognise the difficulty this can cause for the smaller call centre but if this difficulty can be overcome the benefits can be substantial.

Many public programmes for call centre team leaders are no doubt very good and may have to suffice rather than not train at all.

However, if possible the training should be done in-house, using the services of a consultant if necessary. The content of a team leader training programme should cover the areas and subjects identified above.

Other considerations in training

Training for teamworking

We know from our own practical experience of working in different groups that some are more effective than others. Some groups seem to have an almost indefinable quality about them, which makes them different. We usually refer to this quality as teamwork.

Any group of people working together can become a team and experience the benefits which teamworking brings. A team is a group with a difference – it is a higher level, more cohesive gathering of people, which can deliver real improvements in output.

Being part of a team means that you can rely on your colleagues to work with the group's interests at heart. Each individual's self-interests are in union with the interests of the team. Members recognise that as part of the team they can be stronger and more effective.

Getting to this stage does not happen by accident – it has to be planned and worked for. Most importantly, however, it has to be worked for on the job and in the work environment, not during team-building events. Of course, such team-building events have an important part to play. They help to raise awareness and can provide a 'safe' environment for people to experiment with different behaviours. They can also help people to see what teamworking could mean for themselves and their colleagues. But team-building events, no matter how good, are not a magic formula. Sending a group away for a weekend of team-building will not make them into a team. It may create an awareness of what it could be like to work in a team, but this then has to be followed up in the working environment if a team is to be built.

Building teams in work

It is useful to think about what a team is – what does it do differently that makes it a team? It is possible to identify a number of characteristics which teams are likely to display and which appear to be important for working together as a team. These include:

- *clear and agreed objectives* – everyone understands and is committed to the team's objectives and each person's best efforts are attuned to the team purpose;

- *shared vision and values* – everyone instinctively knows how the team and each individual member would respond to a particular decision or a situation;

- *clear definition of responsibilities* – everyone works towards achieving their responsibilities in a cooperative and flexible way;

- *open and honest communication* – within the team and with the team leader.

A team also:

- *encourages growth* – everyone in the team is committed to development for themselves and their colleagues;

- *responds well to challenging performance standards* – effective teams respond well to a challenge;

- *has a supportive, blame-free atmosphere* – people can feel relaxed about taking risks; everyone's contribution is received openly and disagreements are examined and resolved;

- *makes most decisions by agreement* – with each person accepting the agreed course of action, even though they may have challenged it while it was under discussion;

- *achieves synergy* – by combining everyone's differing strengths in such a way that their output as a team exceeds the sum of their individual outputs;

- *continually improves by learning from experience* – reviewing its performance in order to build on successes and prevent failures happening in future;

- *is fun to belong to* – people enjoy themselves and can relax with each other;

- *has a high win rate* – even with exacting tasks its success is likely to be sustained – success breeds success.

There is no one clear way of building a team – though clearly some behaviours are more likely to contribute to success than others. Those wanting to build teams in call centres should review the above characteristics and explore how they can be encouraged within their teams. They will also want to consider the role of training in opening up the thinking and awareness of the group to the possibility and benefits of becoming a team.

Management training

Training for managers is essential and the question that has to be confronted is how far is it possible or necessary for managers in call centres to receive training that is different to general training as a manager? In our view much of the training that is necessary for managers in call centres is already covered in many general management programmes concerned with leadership, management style, behaviours, motivation and climate. In addition there are a number of specialist areas that managers in call centres should receive training in. These include:

- *call centre technology* – the technology can be complex and it is important for a manager to understand and be equipped to operate it;

- *managing in a call centre* – there are special issues of managing in call centres many of which we have referred to in this book that managers need to develop understanding and skills in. These include: call monitoring, observation and analysis; management information systems; and the analysis of statistics covering call volume and information about how time on calls is used.

Finding the right programmes

The difficulty faced by many call centre managers is where to find this training, as only in larger organisations will such programmes be developed and run in-house. Many, perhaps the majority, have to look for public programmes which can offer significant benefits but which are often not sufficiently targeted to meet the needs of many managers. If even a small number of managers in an organisation would benefit from training in some of the specialist areas of call centre management we suggest that a conversation with the organisers of public programmes may lead to them being able to help by adapting the contents of a programme to meet some specific needs. Alternatively the investment in asking a specialist trainer to work with a small number should be explored. For training in technology there is no reason why managers should not participate in training with call centre agents.

Checklist of key actions

- Training of agents and team leaders will contribute significantly to the efficiency and success of a call centre

- It is essential to analyse training needs taking account of:

    - the needs of the organisation;

- the needs of individual agents.

- Recognise that some training is essential including:

  - induction training;

  - building customer contact skills;

  - getting the most out of the technology;

  - developing team leader skills.

- Other important training which should not be ignored includes:

  - training for teamworking;

  - training in management/supervisory skills.

CHAPTER 5

Managing performance

Why are call centres different?

In conducting research that assisted our preparation for writing this book we spoke to a large number of managers, many working in call centres and some who, while not working in a call centre, interact regularly with them. One of the areas we wanted to explore was the frequently asked question: 'Is managing people in a call centre different to managing people in other parts of a business?' Many managers, including some who work in call centres, stated that, in their opinion, the differences are limited. Others, probably a majority, claimed that there are significant differences which managers in call centres need to take into account when planning a strategy for performance management. We came to the view that it is in the application of management that the need for more specialist skills is required.

A major difference in relation to performance management is that the technology in use in most call centres makes the possibility of managing and measuring the performance of employees more precise and objective. This technology, while providing significantly more information about the performance of an individual employee, also places on the manager/team leader a much greater responsibility to assist people to improve performance. It is unfortunately true that far too few managers in all organisations devote time to helping employees improve their performance. If only more managers spent time coaching employees in the day-to-day skills required for superior performance, the performance of many individuals would greatly increase.

In a call centre the manager has at his/her fingertips a range of technology which enables constant measurement of, for example:

- the number of calls, in or out, an agent makes;

- the time spent on each call;

- the wrap-up time;

- the down time;

- the speed of response to each call;

- the effectiveness of the call measured by the strike rate or achievement of the preferred outcome;

- the quality of the calls in delivering the messages required.

Each of these approaches to measuring performance provides the manager/team leader with an array of accurate, up-to-date information that can be used to assess performance.

It is not, however, the availability of information that makes for successful performance management, but what a manager does with the information once he or she has it. It is our contention that knowing how well people are doing is only the starting point for performance management and that what really matters is how the manager uses the information to help each individual to improve their performance. Achieving improved performance should be easier in a call centre as a result of the availability of more objective information about performance. Many would argue, though, that it is more difficult because of the problem of taking people away from the telephone for training and coaching.

However, if performance management is about improving and not just measuring performance, managers and team leaders must make time for enabling performance improvement.

,

Helping people achieve performance improvement

It is generally true that performance improvement is mainly achieved in two ways:

- helping people to maintain/improve their desire and motivation to succeed;

- helping people to enhance their skill and application to enable them to improve performance.

A manager or team leader can help with the first by providing regular motivational feedback and with the latter by providing formative feedback and coaching.

Delivering effective motivational feedback

Everyone, no matter at what level they are in an organisation, can benefit from receiving recognition and encouragement. Everyone needs to know how well they are doing and being told when they are doing well helps them to identify the successful behaviour, repeat it, build it into the way they work and in many cases go on to achieve even more.

Managers and team leaders who want to deliver more motivational feedback should follow the checklist below.

Checklist for delivering motivational feedback

- Identify clearly the desired performance behaviour. Which activities or behaviours do you really want to recognise:

  - speed

  - accuracy

  - friendliness

  - timeliness

  - teamworking

  - taking extra care

  and so on.

- Once you have identified those elements in a job, which deliver superior performance, communicate them clearly to all concerned.

- When you observe an individual doing any of these in a superior way tell them you are pleased/impressed with the way they handled that call, customer or colleague.

- Give the recognition as soon as possible after you have observed the activity or behaviour you want to recognise.

- Give the recognition in public. It is good for others to know that you recognise people for their efforts.

- Make the recognition specific. The more clearly the activity or behaviour being recognised can be identified the easier it will be to persuade the employee to repeat it. There is a place for generalised recognition but specific feedback is more effective.

- Motivational feedback should be delivered in a clear, positive, sincere and confident way. Delivering motivational feedback in a hesitant, unclear, joking way can detract from the benefit and people may not believe it is sincere.

- Do it often and your ability to deliver it in a motivating way will improve.

- If it is not sincere don't do it.

Be careful not to detract from the motivational impact of the feedback by adding a 'but' and then going on to give formative or corrective feedback. For example: *'You handled that call very well and really put that customer at ease, but if you had only asked more open questions you might have closed the sale.'*

There is a time for delivering feedback in this way but it is not appropriate when delivering motivational feedback. It can be useful when it is the opening element in formative feedback, which then leads on to coaching for improved performance. If you want to use the feedback for the purpose of motivation deliver the specific 'well done' and leave it at that.

Delivering effective formative feedback

Formative feedback is designed to go beyond recognising performance and actually intervene in a positive way with a view to helping the individual to improve their performance.

Formative feedback should be given when the manager is confident that the employee can improve once they realise that improvement is possible and knows how to achieve it.

Giving formative feedback places a responsibility on the manager or team leader to help the individual identify how to improve. This second step usually means that the manager devotes time to coaching. The following checklist will help managers improve their skill in giving formative feedback.

Checklist for delivering formative feedback

- Open up a discussion with the employee about the possibility of improving a particular activity or behaviour. This can be done easily during a regular review of performance or soon after the activity in question has been identified.

- Make it specific. The more clearly the activity or behaviour you believe they can improve can be described the easier it will be to get them to focus on the actions for improvement that are required.

- Do not save up formative feedback for appraisal or other review sessions, unless they are held weekly. When a potential performance improvement is postponed it reinforces the activity or behaviour, can make it more difficult to change and continues to contribute to lower productivity.

- Discuss the under-performance with the individual but remember the importance of self-appraisal in gaining commitment to change. Self-appraisal can help you to get the other person to open up and approach the discussion in a way, which will help learning and progress.

Self-appraisal

Think about how you feel when someone says '*I was disappointed with the way you did that. It didn't work out very well.*' Contrast this with your feeling when asked *'How did you feel about that? Were you pleased with the outcome?'*

The first comment is likely to result in barriers being created and the individual feeling they have to defend. The second comment allows the individual to be more honest both with themselves and with, the other person. It is a more open and genuinely enquiring question likely to encourage a more open response. Applying this to giving formative feedback means that it helps if you ask the other person how they rate their performance before telling them what you think. This means that a clear focus on improvement becomes possible and the feedback can be used more positively.

Once the possibility of improvement has been opened up in this way it is much easier to go on to coaching.

Coaching for improved performance

When acting in the role of a coach the manager or team leader is responsible for the development of the learner. Coaching is a process of helping. However, nothing a coach can do will change the behaviour of another person. Everyone is responsible for their own behaviour. Another person (a coach) can help an individual to change, advise them on the most appropriate changes and help them develop knowledge, skill and behaviour that will enable them to change.

In practice this means, the learner has to deepen knowledge and understanding independently, but with the guidance of the coach. Through a guided learning process a better learning success is gained and the learner is more likely to adopt this behaviour in his or her working environment and develop independent working skills.

A change in attitude always becomes possible after a change in behaviour!

Coaching is a process. The optimising of behaviour and the development of new problem-solving skills takes time.

This means that, when acting as a coach, you have to guide the learner in each phase of the process. As a coach you set the framework for the learning, beginning with clarification of the behaviour, skill or attitude you have jointly agreed needs to change.

Coaching is not:

- telling someone exactly how to do something;
- giving instructions laying down specific guidelines about how to accomplish a particular task;
- setting boundaries;
- setting targets for the learner.

Coaching is:

- creating a climate in which improved performance becomes not only possible but desirable;

- helping;

- guiding;

- encouraging;

- getting the learner to own targets which are they themselves have set;

- helping the learner to explore options.

Role of the learner:

- The learner must play an active part in the learning process.

- The learner is responsible for his or her own learning success.

- The learner builds up trust in the coach to create an effective learning environment. In this environment the learner should feel comfortable to ask the coach for help when needed.

> The main point of coaching for the learner is that
> the learner is responsible for his/her own learning success!

The learner benefits through:

- more effective learning

- greater challenge leading to greater achievement

- more self-confidence.

Role of the coach:

A coach is *not* a teacher and does *not* have a controlling function over the learner. (Of course the manager/team leader when operating as a coach retains a controlling function over the learner, but coaching works best when the manager acts as a coach, not as a manager.)

The manager (coach) sets the framework for the learning process. He or she helps the learner to explore alternatives and offers support and encouragement, but the application of the change remains with the learner.

Active support and motivation are the main tasks of the coach!

Communication and involvement

We referred elsewhere in this book to the importance of training for call centre agents, supervisors and managers and we stressed the vital role training has to play in contributing to success. In addition to training, however, effective call centre management requires a clear plan of action for regular communication with agents.

All communication should be designed to inform, educate or motivate. It should be as immediate and as accessible to those receiving it as possible.

There are a number of special issues within the management of call centres, which have to be taken into account when designing an approach to communication. Two in particular relate to the relationship of the call centre to the organisation.

1. The ability of a call centre agent to communicate up-to-date information to customers is an essential element in building customer confidence. For this to happen communication and marketing management within the organisation needs to ensure that a facility for rapid updating of call centre agents exists. Almost nothing can be more damaging to customer confidence than the customer realising that they know more about a new product or process than the agent they are talking to.

2. Call centres are frequently sited a long way from the organisation's traditional centre of operation, meaning that it is easy to leave them out of the communication loop. Many are designed to be so self-managing as to be frequently overlooked by senior management. As a consequence agents may feel they work for the call centre and have little or no

relationship to the parent organisation, let alone act as a key element in adding value.

In addition there are a number of issues within call centres that managers should be aware of when thinking about communication and the involvement of employees:

- The job of the manager in a call centre can be one long round of firefighting, attempting to solve everyday problems in a reactive way. Such may be the day-to-day pressures that few managers have time to step back and focus on the need to ensure that communication to agents is taking place. A consequence of this can be that the responsibility for communication is delegated to people who may lack the skills, understanding or information to carry it out effectively. Even worse, it may be overlooked completely.

- The nature of work in call centres also creates problems for communication. The immediacy of the customer contact, the overwhelming need to answer the ringing telephone, shift working and the organisation of teams – all contribute to the special problem of making communication work.

The examples cited above are not the only issues of communication that call centre managers have to deal with but they do serve to emphasise that if management recognises the need for a well informed, motivated and involved workforce they have to work at achieving it.

Designing communication that works

Many people doubt the importance of communication because they fail to see its relevance to more effective working and the contribution it can make to the overall success of the organisation or unit. However, information gained from employee attitude surveys consistently identifies the importance of communication as one of the important factors contributing to overall employee satisfaction and effectiveness. Effective communication delivers a number of benefits including:

- improved involvement of the individual with the organisation as a whole;

- better understanding and commitment to the core values and objectives of the organisation;

- greater personal ownership of the work people do;

- improved productivity;

- reduced employee turnover;

- better teamworking;

- more responsiveness to customer needs.

Each of these is important in achieving effectiveness in a call centre. In developing an approach to communication it is important to clarify what it is you want to achieve and set clear objectives to enable the effectiveness of the communication to be measured. Most of all it is important to understand that regular and effective communication with all employees is an essential management activity, not an optional extra.

In designing a plan for communication it is worth separating it into the following broad categories:

• communication with and from the operational centre;

• communication within the call centre.

Communication with the operational centre

The nature of the work in call centres means that all agents must be kept up to date with organisational developments, particularly those that have an impact on the customer. The technology, which is available in many call centres can make this type of instant communication easier.

Information about product or policy changes can be swiftly updated and made available to agents easily and quickly via the Internet or intranet. To make this type of information stick, many organisations increasingly use broadcast standard messages which include film and animation in addition to simple text. This enhanced packaging of the message makes it more memorable as well as easy for individual agents to take on board.

Company information, activities and developments as well as communication about the core values and objectives of the organisation can be communicated in the same way. Interest and involvement can be stimulated by local organisation of quizzes, short presentations and discussions designed to reinforce the messages previously received.

Involvement, commitment and a sense of belonging to the organisation can also be stimulated by regular contact with senior management. Call centres tend to be at the edge of the company empire and off the beaten track. This can mean that senior managers may find it easier not to visit than visit. However, it is recognised that the amount of contact and interest managers show in the day-to-day operation of the business delivers a big payoff in relation to employee motivation. Such visits should not, however, consist of wearing a hole in the carpet between the door and the manager's office. They have to be occasions during which the visiting manager interacts with, talks and, more importantly, listens to the agents. It is easy to underestimate the value and importance of helping call centre agents to feel and act as part of the larger organisation. In financial services, for example, few if any senior managers would regard the people employed in a branch office as not being fully part of the organisation. Rather, the people working in branches are recognised as being the main point of contact with the customers of the organisation and a key element in the retail supply chain.

However, in relation to the way many call centres are treated, it would be easy to gain the impression that people at the operational centre believe them to be part of a separate organisation offering specialist services. Unfortunately few, if any, senior managers operating at the centre of many organisations have any experience of working in call centres. This means for many that the importance of the role of the call centre has not yet been clearly identified.

We strongly recommend that managers rethink the importance of call centres and recognise them not only as a way of reducing costs but as a key link with customers – in many cases the only link – and an essential element in the retail supply chain. When this is done more call centres will be drawn into a closer relationship with their parent organisations.

Communication within the call centre

Effective communication leads to improved performance but in order to be effective, communication has to be planned. It must happen consistently and it must be clear to all concerned why it is happening.

We suggest that a consistent approach to communication in a call centre should include each of the following vehicles:

- readerboards;

- huddles;

- team briefings;

- the manager's listening hour;

- town hall meetings.

We outline below each of these vehicles in more detail.

Readerboards

Traditionally one of the main vehicles of communication in call centres has been the readerboard and while this will continue to be an important element, it is important to recognise its limitations. The readerboard can display up-to-date information about current activity and, most importantly, about achievement against objectives and targets. It can also be a valuable motivational tool, stimulating agents to improve turnaround times or increase sales.

Readerboards unfortunately can also act as a demotivator for some people. Team leaders should keep a close watch on how

---

people are responding to information contained on the readerboard. They should make sure that if the information appears to be having a negative affect on an individual they should act to reassure that individual as quickly as possible. Readerboards are intended to motivate and stimulate and they work effectively in achieving this but they are only a tool and management has to use them wisely if they are to be effective.

This can be done by regularly reviewing the information displayed in order to make sure that it is both relevant and doing what it is designed to do.

Huddles

A huddle is a short, stand-up meeting held at the start of every shift. A huddle should be held every day for every team. A huddle is designed to inform and motivate team members. They should last for no more than six or seven minutes and the content should cover:

- how well the team did yesterday;

- what needs to be done differently, if anything;

- what we plan to do today;

- what issues may impact on this;

- anything special about today, for example the birthday of a team member, outside visitors on site, etc.;

- what they need to do to achieve their objectives for the day.

It is essential that team leaders lead the huddle and deliver the messages in an upbeat way – huddles should be fun, and if they become boring they fail to achieve their primary objectives of informing and motivating the team. The outcome of a huddle should be that all participants are enthusiastic owners of the information gained.

Team briefings

The team briefing should be held either weekly or monthly. If a daily huddle is held it is likely that a team briefing held monthly will be sufficient. The purpose of the team briefing is to draw together all the activities of the call centre and the team during the past month and inform participants about strategy plans and objectives for the future. The briefing should help to develop pride in the organisation at both a corporate and local level.

They should take place in the work area and should last for approximately 30 minutes. The content should include:

- updates on performance and developments in the unit and the team since the last meeting;

- important corporate messages that people need to be aware of;

- important local messages that people need to be aware of;

- an open discussion involving team members getting feedback about their views and opinions;

- future plans for the unit and the organisation;

- a motivational message from the team leader or manager.

Team briefings should inform and motivate participants. They should always include an opportunity for questions and discussion between participants as well as between participants and the team leader.

The team leader should:

- be enthusiastic;

- be open to accepting alternative opinions;

- ask open questions;

- be a good listener;

- be positive;

- be able to demonstrate commitment to the process.

The manager's listening hour

A manager's listening hour is just what it says, once every two or three months senior managers devote one hour to listening to the views and opinions of a group of their people. (In a small call centre it may be advisable for the listening hour to be held less frequently.)

Ideally the group should consist of some12 people drawn from a cross section of the call centre. Participants should be changed from month to month, although some overlap can be useful for discussing follow-ups.

The agenda should be open and largely dictated by the participants, although, of course, management may want to test out ideas from time to time. Be careful with this, as if the agenda is perceived to be dictated by management, people will soon lose interest. Participants should be allowed to discuss anything they want, although some organisations deliberately outlaw discussion on issues such as pay negotiations which are dealt with by a separate body. This works well providing that people are fully informed beforehand. Participants are not 'representatives' in a formal sense although they should be 'representative' of the employees as a whole, i.e. not drawn from any particular section or identifiable group.

When first established a manager's listening hour may feel like providing people with an opportunity for a moan, because people *will* moan, but the sensitive manager will be able to turn this into obtaining greater insight by careful questioning. The sceptical manager needs to remember that it is in the interest of everyone to be aware of and in a position to tackle issues of irritation to staff early and a listening hour provides an ideal opportunity to do this.

If a 'listening hour' does appear to be a moaning session, we recommend that the manager should stick with it – let the moaning work itself out and gradually move the agenda on to identifying and discussing other things.

A listening hour can also provide positive insight into potential improvements in areas of quality, performance, working practice and policy across the entire call centre.

The following guidelines can help you make sure your listening hour works:

- Restrict the time to one hour.

- No more than one or two managers should attend.

- Always use a flipchart to capture feedback, ideas and opinions.

- Record any decisions clearly.

- Listen carefully and show interest in everything that is said.

- Ask questions to clarify and involve.

The results and outcomes of the meeting – ideas and actions agreed upon – should be available to everyone. Many organisations display them on general notice boards.

If there are positive outcomes identified and agreed it is important to act on them as quickly as possible. Nothing will destroy the benefits of a 'listening hour' more quickly than a feeling that they are all about talk with no action.

Town hall meetings

A town hall meeting is an opportunity for senior management to meet with and communicate directly to everyone who works in the call centre. They should be held every four or six months and as well as being an opportunity to bring everyone up to date about developments they can be used to celebrate success. Give awards and recognition for superior performance to involve and motivate. They should involve as many people as possible. Some will argue that the nature of the work in a call centre makes it difficult to get everyone together; others say that the nature of the work presents a challenge to be overcome.

To gain maximum coverage it may be necessary for the managers leading the meeting to be on site for every shift for two or three days. If this is unusual it can have a very positive impact on people who work unsocial hours to see senior managers in this environment.

We heard in our research of a new chief executive of an organisation who committed himself to visiting every location and every shift within his first three months. He did this successfully and as a result has created a real feeling of how he values the contribution of everyone to the success of the business.

It is our experience that town hall meetings can be a very effective way of helping senior managers to keep in touch with opinions and feelings in the unit. They also provide an opportunity for managers to communicate strategy, paint the big picture and inspire people.

Leadership and management style

Success in any management job requires recognition that people are the most important asset. Many people say this but only the really effective manager puts it into action. Only through a combination of many individuals' efforts and achievements can ongoing progress be made towards the accomplishment of organisational goals.

Management in a call centre is a classic example of a working environment that requires a commitment to getting the best out of the people, for the success of the call centre depends entirely on the effectiveness of its people.

To get the best from people the manager must help them not only to work better as individuals but also to cooperate together as a team. Everyone in a managerial position at whatever level has a pivotal role to play in ensuring that the energy and talents of all the people are released towards continually improving performance. This means as managers and leaders they have to make sure that their actions are geared to ensuring that people get the support and encouragement they need.

Be a leader not just a manager

A manager has a responsibility for leadership by virtue of their position. But whether they act as a leader in the true sense of the word depends on how they behave. A manager can be appointed but a leader must earn the respect of people for leadership to be possible. It is useful to think about leadership in this way because it helps us understand that an individual may:

- be a leader by designation only – they are not actually acting as a leader;

- act as an unofficial leader – fulfilling the role of leader as well as the official designated leader.

To manage means to have authority, to take charge of, to direct and to control. To lead means to guide, to help, to support, to encourage and, most of all, to influence and to develop. Good managers are able to master systems, procedures and practices. Good leaders have the insight and judgement to question whether the system or procedure should exist at all, and see how it could be improved. It has been said that management is about efficiency, while leadership is about effectiveness.

Clearly both management and leadership are important. To succeed in combining the two means putting the leadership activities first. In other words, think first about effectiveness – about applying the correct priorities and giving them attention. Only then should attention be paid to efficiency – choosing the most appropriate way of performing a task. There is little point in being highly efficient about the wrong things.

Nowhere is this more apparent than in call centres. Only through getting the best out of people will the organisation be able to succeed in the highly competitive world that call centres operate in.

Checklist of key actions

- A manager in a call centre has access to a range of technology that enables the measurement of performance. It is important to take full advantage of this information.

- The ability to give feedback, both motivational and formative, is an essential skill for managing in a call centre.

- Coaching people to improve their skills has a direct impact on business performance.

- The effective implementation of a consistent approach to communication will enhance the involvement of agents and help to increase motivation and awareness.

- Communication within the call centre should be planned, regular and consistent.

- Managers and team leaders in call centres must develop and display effective leadership skills.

CHAPTER 6

Conclusions

An important debate surrounding managing people in call centres is the issue about whether or not management is different in a call centre from management in other environments. We have made reference to this issue at various times in this book and we broadly take the view that many of the lessons learned in more traditional environments can be used to inform the approach to management in a call centre.

However, there are special circumstances in the call centre environment which require different approaches to deal with the special needs of people in call centres.

Managers in call centres need to be aware that people working in call centres are 'knowledge workers' – individuals who use their brains, emotions and thinking processes in their work. Much of the work of an agent may be repetitive and the working environment may be cramped. However, when the individual agent is interacting with a customer she or he is the company representative and has a major influence in determining the relationship the customer has with the company. They have in their hands, or perhaps more correctly in their voice, the potential to influence business success or failure.

Research increasingly shows that the retention and motivation of 'knowledge workers' will be a key issue for management in the future. The costs associated with replacing experienced people are growing daily, and potentially even more damaging to a business is the loss of knowledge and experience which goes with an agent when they leave.

Of course, there will always be turnover and we would not argue for organisations to seek to create a situation of nil turnover. We would, however, suggest that as knowledge becomes more important – as it does every day in call centres – retention should be a key concern for management.

We referred earlier in the book to why people leave and indicated that pay is only one element out of many why people do so. A fact that is well known but seldom acted upon is that people leave managers, not companies, and nowhere is this more true than in call centres, where the nature of the work demands a supportive approach to managing people.

Call centre managers need to be aware that 'knowledge workers' in particular need from their manager:

- a clear understanding of what is expected of them;

- help through training and management support in developing the skills necessary to achieve success;

- positive recognition and feedback when they are doing well and positive formative feedback to help them improve things when they do less well;

- a manager who takes an interest, who shows concern and, most of all, who does what she or he says she or he will do.

Managers in call centres need to 'walk the talk' if they are to be successful at managing people. They need to understand that their success can only be achieved through the agents with whom they work.

The way a call centre is managed, and in particular the way leadership is demonstrated, has a significant influence on the business success, or not, of the call centre. Effective managers are aware of this and ensure that they provide the leadership necessary to achieve success.

Monitoring performance quality

A sample assessment form

The forms on the following pages should be used to assess the performance quality of agents.

The process

Step 1

You should record and assess three consecutive calls and complete the performance quality assessment form immediately after carrying out the assessment.

You should base your assessment on the following scoring system:

---

1   Exceeds expectations

2   Performance acceptable

3   Some development needs identified

4   Significant development needs identified

Remember that when making your assessment you should be looking to identify specific information that will be helpful for the agent when giving them feedback. Avoid phrases such as *'you did it very well'*; use instead phrases such as *'the question you asked during the opening of the conversation put the customer at ease quickly.'* Specific descriptive feedback is always more helpful than generalised comments.

Step 2

Feedback should be given to the agent as soon as possible after you have made the assessment.

Guidelines for assessment

Opening the call: company identification, greeting, friendliness, politeness and security check.

Establishing the needs: identifying customer needs and summarising to demonstrate understanding.

Solutions: was a viable and acceptable solution offered to the customer? If the agent could not identify a correct solution was the call correctly referred?

Use of the system: competence demonstrated in using the system.

Communication skills: questioning and listening – were effective questions used to establish needs and facts? Did the agent interrupt the customer? Did the agent use the customer's name?

Telephone skills: did the agent demonstrate confidence and professionalism? Was a smooth pace achieved? Did the agent respond positively to the customer avoiding the use of jargon?

Closing the call: was the close positive and polite? Was the customer's name used? Was further help and information offered?

Company awareness: did the agent demonstrate company and product knowledge, identify sales leads and correctly refer the customer if appropriate?

Giving feedback and agreeing training needs

Complete the feedback and training needs section of the form and agree how any additional training will be delivered and a date for review.

Remember always to start with the strengths and make sure you identify some positive aspects of the performance.

Assessment form

Name of agent		
Name of team leader		
Date of assessment		
Date of feedback		
Subject	**Score**	**Comment**
Opening the call		
Establishing the Needs		
Solutions		
Use of the system		
Communication skills		
Telephone skills		
Closing the call		
Company awareness		

Feedback and training plan

Strengths
Development needs
How will these be met?
Specific training needs
How will these be met?
Date of review